A Brief Introduction
to the Philosophy of Mind

A BRIEF INTRODUCTION
TO THE PHILOSOPHY OF MIND

by
NEIL CAMPBELL

broadview guides to philosophy

Library and Archives Canada Cataloguing in Publication

Campbell, Neil, 1967–
    A brief introduction to the philosophy of mind / by Neil Campbell.

(Broadview guides to philosophy)
Includes bibliographical references and index.
ISBN 1-55111-617-0
    1. Philosophy of mind. I. Title. II. Series.

BD418.3.C34 2004   128'.2   C2004-905507-0

Broadview Press Ltd. is an independent, international publishing house, incorporated in 1985. Broadview believes in shared ownership, both with its employees and with the general public; since the year 2000 Broadview shares have traded publicly on the Toronto Venture Exchange under the symbol BDP.

We welcome comments and suggestions regarding any aspect of our publications–please feel free to contact us at the addresses below or at broadview@broadviewpress.com / www.broadviewpress.com

North America
PO Box 1243, Peterborough, Ontario, Canada K9J 7H5
Tel: (705) 743-8990; Fax: (705) 743-8353
email: customerservice@broadviewpress.com
3576 California Road, Orchard Park, NY, USA 14127

UK, Ireland, and continental Europe
NBN Plymbridge
Estover Road
Plymouth PL6 7PY UK
Tel: 44 (0) 1752 202 301
Fax: 44 (0) 1752 202 331
Fax Order Line: 44 (0) 1752 202 333
Customer Service: cservs@nbnplymbridge.com
Orders: orders@nbnplymbridge.com

Australia and New Zealand
UNIREPS, University of New South Wales
Sydney, 2052
Australia
Tel: 61 2 9664 0999; Fax: 61 2 9664 5420
email: info.press@unsw.edu.au

Edited by Betsy Struthers

Broadview Press Ltd. gratefully acknowledges the financial support of the Government of Canada through the Book Publishing Industry Development Program for our publishing activities.

PRINTED IN CANADA

To my mother, Janis Hoogstraten,
whose love and support has made
all the difference in the world.

Contents

■ PREFACE

This text is designed for use in introductory courses in the philosophy of mind. It can be used either as the primary text or, ideally, as a companion to a collection of readings. Philosophy of mind is an intriguing part of philosophy, but the central works are often dense and philosophically advanced, for they were not written with the typical undergraduate student in mind. Thus, there is a genuine need for a text that can guide students through the philosophical terrain and offer clear explanations of the central theories and debates that make up this fascinating topic. My hope is that this text will fill this need. Since the central mind-body theories are covered, this book should be a fine complement to virtually any anthology or custom-made collection of readings. I hope you have as much fun reading this book as I had writing it.

I would like to express my gratitude to the fine people who work at Broadview Press for making the production of this book a smooth and enjoyable process. I would also like to thank Frances Brennan and my colleagues Rocky Jacobsen and Byron Williston for their very helpful comments on drafts of the chapters in this book.

INTRODUCTION

There are few philosophical problems as captivating as the mind-body problem. More than most others, this problem goes to the very heart of our being, for it not only deals with questions about what kind of beings we are but has profound implications for the issue of immortality. The mind-body problem is generated by two fairly simple observations. The first is that we all have bodies and that our bodies are not a complete mystery to science. We believe that science has a great deal to tell us about how our bodies function and what they are made of. Furthermore, although there are distinct differences in complexity, we tend to think that our bodies are not *fundamentally* different from other physical objects in the world around us, such as chairs, rocks, or trees. Secondly, we also have minds. We think, feel, dream, desire, and engage in a variety of other mental activities. In this respect, we *are* different from most of the physical objects we encounter on a daily basis. Chairs, rocks, and trees are not conscious; they don't think, feel, dream, or have desires of any kind. The mind-body problem concerns the nature of the relationship between these two aspects of our nature: between our thinking selves and our physical selves.

Three Aspects of the Mind-Body Problem

To speak of the mind-body problem as though it were a single problem is somewhat misleading. It is actually a cluster of philosophical issues that fall into three broad categories. The first, and most significant, is the **ontological problem**. Ontology is the study of being, of what there is in the universe. The ontological problem is concerned with the question: *what kind of thing is a human being?* It explores whether we are merely complex physical bodies or whether we also have non-physical minds or souls in addition to our bodies. Second is the **epistemological problem**. Epistemology is the study of knowledge; it explores how we acquire knowledge and what the differences are between knowledge and opinion. In the context of the mind-body problem, the epistemological problem examines questions about our knowledge of other minds, such as: *How do we know what other people think, feel, or believe? How do we know that other people have minds?* These are difficult questions because a person's mental states seem to be a very different kind of thing from their physical traits. For example, we can determine if someone is right- or left-handed by watching them sign their name or drink a glass of water, but we cannot so easily know what a person thinks, feels, or believes, especially if that person is private about their thoughts and feelings. We cannot simply *observe* what another person believes in the way we can observe that another person is left-handed. The third category is the **semantic problem**. Semantics is the study of meaning, and so the semantic problem is concerned with how words that refer to mental states like "pain" acquire their meaning. Philosophers interested in this kind of question wonder whether the word "pain" refers to an essentially private sensation (the way pain feels to the person who feels it), or if it gets its meaning from publicly observable phenomena such as behaviour (saying "Ouch!") and the conditions under which that behaviour occurs (after bodily damage, for instance).

To divide the mind-body problem into three categories is not to imply that these issues are neatly compartmentalized. In fact, there is a great deal of overlap. Thus, sometimes views on epistemological or semantic problems are used to motivate conclusions about the ontological problem, and vice versa. It is therefore more appropriate to think of these three categories as being interrelated. Although this book will touch on all aspects of the mind-body problem, its primary focus is the ontological problem. Our main task will be to examine and evaluate various competing **theories of mind**: philosophical solutions to the ontological problem that attempt to explain the nature of our mental states. Among other things, a theory of mind asks whether our thoughts and sensations are non-physical states of some kind or whether they are physical phenomena. If a theory claims that mental states are non-physical states, it has to explain how these non-physical states are related to our physical bodies. Alternatively, if a theory says that mental states are physical states, it needs to explain what kinds of physical phenomena our mental states really are. Before we can survey the philosophical terrain on this issue, it will be useful to illuminate a few concepts. Let's start by clarifying what philosophers mean by **mental states.**

Mental States

In one sense you already know perfectly well what mental states are: psychological attributes and occurrences such as thoughts, feelings, perceptions, desires, doubts, and imaginings, to name just a few examples. However, philosophers have identified several characteristics possessed by mental states with which you might not be familiar. For instance, you probably never noticed that mental states like these can be divided into two kinds, which philosophers call **propositional attitudes** and **qualitative states of consciousness.**

Propositional attitudes are mental states like beliefs, desires, and doubts. These are grouped together because all such mental states have a common structure: they all involve a psychological attitude that is directed toward a state of affairs described by a proposition. This sounds complicated but is actually quite simple. Let's think about beliefs for a moment. If you say to someone that you have a belief, they will inevitably ask you *what* you believe. This is because you never simply believe. When you have a belief, there is always *something that you believe.* This something that you believe is some state of affairs or other, such as the way the world is or might be. For example, you can believe that *the summer is rapidly coming to an end.* The same thing is true for desires and doubts. You cannot simply desire and doubt, you have to desire or doubt *something*. For example, you can desire that *you don't have to go back to school* or doubt that *it will be a warm fall*. In each case, what follows the word "that" is a description of a state of affairs expressed in the form of a **proposition**. The states of affairs these propositions describe (i.e., *what* you believe, desire, or doubt) are called their **propositional contents**. Beliefs, desires, and doubts, then, are called propositional attitudes because they involve the adoption of an attitude (believing, desiring, doubting) toward a proposition (*what* you believe, desire, or doubt).

Qualitative states of consciousness include mental states such as feelings, sensations, perceptions, and emotions. It is common knowledge that we use our senses to gain information about the world around us. For instance, you might say that you know there is a rose in front of you because you can see it, smell it, feel it, and even taste it if you are so inclined. In each case your knowledge of the rose depends on a sensation. Each of these sensations *feels* to you a certain way. That is, when you touch the petals of a rose, you are aware of a smooth, silky quality. Similarly, when you smell it, you are aware of a certain perfume-like odour; when you look at it, you have a sensation of a certain shade of redness. These are all properties of your sensations of the rose, and it is these properties that you are aware of in your conscious experience. These properties are often called **qualia** or **phenomenal properties**. Other sensations have qualia too. For example, the painfulness of pain, the itchiness of itches, and that peculiar feeling of the sense of losing one's balance are all qualia. *Every* sensory state has qualia of some sort, for every sensory state *feels like something* to its possessor.

The qualitative states of consciousness are quite different from propositional attitudes. The former have a certain kind of feeling associated with them, whereas the latter do not. It does not feel like anything to *doubt* or *believe* that it is going to snow, whereas it does feel like something to *see* snow. To see that this is true, try a little experiment. Try to doubt that the sky is falling. Now doubt that the sun will rise tomorrow. Do you notice any significant difference between how these two doubts *feel*? You probably had trouble making the comparison. The reason for this is most likely that you could not actually compare the feeling of the two doubts because you couldn't isolate a particular feeling that was associated with either one of them. That is, you could not identify what it feels like to doubt that the sky is falling, and you could not identify what it feels like to doubt that the sun will rise tomorrow. Since neither of these mental states feels like anything, it is impossible to compare them.

When you doubted that the sky is falling, you might have said silently to yourself, "I doubt the sky is falling" in which case you may think that what it feels like to have this doubt is just to hear an internal monologue that says those words and similarly for doubting that the sun will rise tomorrow. The problem with this strategy is that there are many different ways to formulate the proposition "I doubt the sky is falling." The very same doubt can be expressed by saying "I don't think it is likely that the sky is falling" or even "Je doute que le ciel tombe." Since there is no one way to express this doubt, there can be no one internal monologue that sounds a certain way to associate with it. Thus, there are no particular qualia associated with any propositional attitude.

Something that qualitative states of consciousness and

propositional attitudes have in common, however, is a feature called **intentionality**: the relation of *aboutness*. The psychologist and philosopher Franz Brentano claimed that this is the defining characteristic of the mental, that is, it is what differentiates the mental from the physical. We already saw that propositional attitudes have propositional content that describes the way the world is or could be. Propositional attitudes, then, are *about* the world. Because beliefs, desires, and other propositional attitudes are always about something, they have this feature of intentionality. Similarly, your qualitative states of consciousness have intentionality because your sensations are sensations *of* things in the world (real or imagined). For instance, your sensations of a rose have intentionality because they are sensations *of* a rose.

Theories of Mind

Now that we know what philosophers are referring to when they talk about mental states we are in a better position to appreciate what a theory of mind tells us about them. I mentioned earlier that a theory of mind tells us about the *nature* of mental states. In general there are two main possibilities here. The first is that mental states are non-physical entities of some kind, perhaps the states of a non-physical soul. If one accepts this view and believes that we have physical bodies in addition to these non-physical mental states, then one advocates a view called **dualism**, which claims that two kinds of things exist in our universe: physical things and non-physical things. As we shall see, there can be several forms of dualism depending on how one thinks that our non-physical minds are related to our physical bodies.

The second possibility is that mental states are physical states of some kind. In this case human beings are considered to be nothing more than very complex physical beings. This view is called **materialism** or **physicalism**. What it means for something to be physical is a complex issue in itself. A common understanding often includes ideas such as occupying three-dimensional space (having length, width, and breadth), being something you can touch, or being divisible into smaller parts. This seems appropriate for most of the material objects we encounter every day like furniture and buildings, but what should we say about things like shadows or electromagnetic fields? Shadows only occupy two-dimensional space, and we can't touch or divide an electromagnetic field in the way we can touch or divide a lump of clay. Should we consider shadows and electromagnetic fields non-physical entities? Most of us would suggest that we should not, but this means that we need to broaden our understanding of what it is for something to be physical.

Although shadows and electromagnetic fields do not share the characteristics we usually associate with matter, they are phenomena that we can *explain* in physical terms. That is, when we say that a shadow is caused by an object preventing light from illuminating a surface, there is nothing left to explain about shadows; there is no mystery about why shadows have the properties they do or why they behave like they do. Similarly, if one knows enough physics and electromagnetic theory, one will appreciate that the nature and behaviour of electromagnetic fields can be completely explained according to physical principles. In light of this we ought to say that something is physical if we can (in principle) explain its behaviour and characteristics using the terms and methods of physical theory. The "in principle" is important here because the physical sciences can change fairly radically over long or short periods of time. We do not want to have to say that prior to electromagnetic theory the attractive force of a magnet was a non-physical phenomenon and became a physical phenomenon only *after* the theory was developed. Such a view is surely absurd. The challenge for physicalism, then, is to shed light on how it is that mental states can be physical phenomena. Just as the physical explanation of a shadow should be able to explain the behaviour and properties of shadows, physicalist theories of mind should be able to explain the behaviour and properties of mental states.

The Approach of This Book

Our critical examination of the competing theories of mind begins with dualism. This is an appropriate place to start for two reasons. The first, as we will see in Chapter 1, is that the mind-body problem as we know it today began when the French philosopher René Descartes formulated the problem and argued in favour of dualism. Thus, dualism is a good place to start in order to give you a sense of the historical development of the mind-body problem. The second reason for beginning with dualism is that most people tend to have at least some affinity for dualism as a theory. Although you may not have thought about the mind-body problem in any great detail before, it is quite likely that at some level you think mind and body are different in an important way. For example, perhaps you have a religious background and have been taught that you have a non-physical, immortal soul. Dualism, then, is a good way to enter into the philosophy of mind because it is a *familiar* view, something you have probably encountered already.

Most of the remaining chapters are devoted to alternative versions of physicalism. These should be regarded primarily as reactions against dualism, and we will examine them roughly in the sequence of their historical development. Each theory offers a different account of what it means to say that mental states are physical phenomena. Although the views presented appear in historical progression, this does not imply that more recent theories are more philosophically sound than earlier ones. Most of the theories discussed in this book are views philosophers still take seriously today. Furthermore, we will come to appreciate that even the most recent versions of physicalism suffer from philosophical inadequacies.

The purpose of this text is not to draw any particular conclusions or to argue in favour of one theory of mind over others. Instead, it is to introduce you to the competing views and to present you with an objective discussion of their strengths and weaknesses. In the end, it is up to you to decide which theories have the most merit. My hope, however, is that if you conclude that one theory is better than the others, your conclusion will be based on sound philosophical reasons and arguments.

C H A P T E R 1

■ DUALISM

Why Start with Descartes?

M ost introductory courses in the philosophy of mind start with Descartes's *Meditations on First Philosophy*. The reason for this is that philosophers generally think Descartes offered the first formulation of the mind-body problem and set the terms for the debate that are relevant to discussions of the issue today. This isn't because philosophers before Descartes didn't think about minds and bodies, but because Descartes formulated the mind-body problem differently than his predecessors. In large part, these differences are due to his unique place in history.

Descartes wrote the *Meditations* in the seventeenth century just as the tremendous changes in the natural sciences initiated by Galileo began to take hold. Prior to this, most science was based on the work of Aristotle, a Greek philosopher who died in 322 BCE and whose views on science and philosophy dominated intellectual discourse in the western world until the seventeenth century. According to Aristotle, the natural world is **teleological** or goal-directed. He thought that everything has a natural end or purpose toward which it strives and called these goals or ends **final causes**. The behaviour of all things could, in his view, be explained in terms of these final causes. For example, he thought the final cause of an acorn is an oak tree—that being an oak is the goal towards which acorns naturally strive. Similarly, the trajectory of a comet can be explained in terms of its final cause: its destination. This is not to say that acorns and comets have goals in the same way we do. They do not form intentions or make plans. Nevertheless, they are, according to Aristotle, reaching toward a particular end in the sense that they each have a particular result toward which they are directed. The natural world, for Aristotle, is full of purpose since all kinds of things (including acorns, comets, and human beings) have natural ends towards which they strive.

The new science of Galileo was largely an attack on final causes. Rather than explaining the behaviour of all things by saying that they are pulled toward some natural end, he proposed that the world is a system governed by impersonal laws that push things along toward no end in particular. That is, the reason a comet has the trajectory it does is not, as Aristotle said, because it has a destination toward which it aims, but is rather because the laws of gravitation, the comet's velocity, its current position, and so on, make the comet act the way it does. Galileo (and later Sir Isaac Newton) envisioned a world that is completely deterministic and can be fully described in mechanical terms. On this view, all things are the way they are because of initial conditions and universal laws of nature, and in light of these factors they cannot be otherwise. Consequently, there is no design in the world, and there are no goals or purposes anywhere in nature.

The interesting thing to note about the shift from Aristotelian final causes to mechanical laws is the contrast this introduced between explanations of physical bodies like comets and explanations of human behaviour. Most of the time human behaviour was explained by talking about mental states, which usually involved goals, ends, or purposes—final causes. For example, if you ask me why I got up just now, I might respond by saying that I am thirsty and want to get something to drink. At the heart of this explanation is a goal or a purpose: getting a drink. This explanation is of the same general form as those Aristotle offered for all natural phenomena. Regardless of whether the subject was human beings, acorns, or comets, explanations of behaviour involved reference to final causes. With the growth of the new science this changed. It became a mistake to talk about the natural world as though it were goal-directed. However, human behaviour continued to be explained in terms of mental states like goals or purposes. Thus, human beings began to seem very different from ordinary physical things like acorns and comets.

Descartes enthusiastically embraced the new science but in doing so faced a novel problem. Minds and bodies appeared to be very different kinds of things because the behaviour of bodies could be explained by mathematical principles whereas the behaviour of minds could be explained only by appealing to final causes. The task, then, was to explain how mind and body are related. Thus, the mind-body problem was born.

Cartesian Dualism

Descartes develops his view of the relation between mind and body in the context of a broader epistemological project. The primary goal of the *Meditations* is to secure absolutely certain foundations to ground all of our knowledge. Think of all the things we know as if they were the different levels of a house. If the knowledge that serves as the foundation for all of the other things we know turns out to be uncertain, then all of our knowledge collapses; everything we thought we knew is thrown into doubt. For this reason, it is very important to ensure that the knowledge at the ground level is secure.

For this solid foundation Descartes invokes his **method of doubt**. Its purpose is to cast all the things he thinks he knows into doubt to see if any knowledge remains. If there are claims Descartes cannot doubt, then there are some things he knows for certain, and these can serve as the foundation for other items of knowledge. Thus, in *Meditation One* Descartes draws our attention to all the ways in which we can fall into error. It is fairly obvious that most of our knowledge of the world around us is derived from sense experience. We say that we know the dog is barking because we can hear him, that the sun is shining because we can see it and feel its warmth on our faces, that fudge is sweet because we can taste it, and so on. What if our senses turn out to be not as reliable as we tend to assume? If they are not reliable guides to knowledge, then we probably know a lot less than we think we do. Descartes gives us a variety of reasons for thinking that we cannot trust our senses. He points out, for instance, that we fall prey to optical illusions, that we cannot tell the difference between dreamt experiences and real ones (at least while we are dreaming), and that we often make mistakes about what we experience. These considerations have the cumulative effect of rendering all of our perceptual knowledge uncertain. In Descartes's view, since we cannot at any time definitively rule out the possibility that we are dreaming, are victims of an illusion, or are simply mistaken about what we perceive, we cannot use perception as a source of knowledge. So long as there is even the slightest chance that I am now dreaming (or the victim of an illusion, etc.), I cannot be certain that I see this page in front of me.

Descartes does not stop here, however, for he also introduces the idea of an evil genius, whose purpose is to widen the scope of what we can doubt. The evil genius is a being who has the power to produce any idea whatsoever in our minds. Thus, perhaps the reason I believe there is a page before me is that the evil genius has caused me to have the sensation of a page when there is, in fact, no page before me. Even worse, perhaps the evil genius has made me think that one plus one equals two when in fact it equals three. Perhaps the evil genius has even made me believe I have a body when, in fact, I do not.

Between the potential for perceptual error and the evil genius there does not appear to be a great deal we can know with certainty. Nevertheless, Descartes claims there are some things that escape the method of doubt. For instance, he knows he exists—at least while he is thinking—because even if an evil genius deceives him about everything else, it must be true that Descartes exists in order to be deceived. He also knows he is a thing that is capable of various mental operations. He knows, for instance, that he can *doubt* since he doubts he has knowledge of the external world. He knows he can *understand* since he understands that his senses might not be as reliable as he thought. He knows he can *imagine* because he imagines an evil genius that deceives him at every turn. He also knows he *has sensations,* since he seems to be aware of his body and of objects in his vicinity through his senses. Of course he doesn't know whether his sensations are caused by the things that seem to be around him or if they are caused by an evil genius, but he can't doubt that he *has* sensations.

It is in the context of these kinds of considerations that Descartes offers his first argument for the claim that mind and body are distinct substances. The argument runs as follows:

> I cannot doubt that I have a mind.
> I can doubt that I have a body.
> Therefore, my mind is distinct from my body.

These premises are clearly true. Descartes cannot doubt he has a mind because any such doubt would be *self-defeating*; doubting requires a mind to do the doubting and so cannot occur without one. The second premise is justified by appealing to the various ways in which he can fall into error (e.g., dreaming). Since Descartes could merely be dreaming that he has a body, or might be deceived by the evil genius into thinking he has one, he cannot be sure he has a body. In the end it may turn out that Descartes does have a body, but in the context of the method of doubt it is rational for him to doubt the existence of his body.

In the argument above Descartes draws on a principle that has since come to be called **Leibniz's Law of the indiscernibility of identicals**. This principle claims that if what appear to be two distinct things are, in fact, identical, then they must share all the same properties or characteristics. Let's consider an example to illustrate this principle at work. Imagine that Carole and Vanessa are discussing their boyfriends. They learn that their boyfriends have the same name, the same physical features, and work in the same building. They may become worried that they are dating the same man. To determine whether or not this is so, the two women compare notes to see if they can discover any differences between their boyfriends. If it turns out that Carole's boyfriend has a mole on his left arm and that Vanessa's does not, then Carole and Vanessa can be sure they are dating different men.

These women have employed Leibniz's Law. The only way it can turn out that they are dating the same man is if everything true of Carole's boyfriend were also true of Vanessa's. As long as there is at least one thing that is true of Carole's boyfriend but not of Vanessa's, the boyfriends must be distinct individuals. This is the kind of reasoning Descartes employs in the argument above. If there is even one property the mind possesses that the body does not, it follows that mind and body must be distinct things. Descartes claims to identify such a property: being doubted. Because the existence of his body can be doubted but the existence of his mind cannot be doubted, he claims it follows that mind and body must be distinct things or substances.

Most philosophers think this argument for substance dualism is flawed. They argue that Descartes does not identify an actual property of his body or his mind when he claims he can doubt the existence of his body but not his mind. The reason for saying this is that doubting is a psychological attitude that a mind has toward something else and not a property of the thing being doubted. For example, I might doubt that Tom will ever repay me the money I lent him, but the doubting is not a property of Tom; it is an activity of my mind. Similarly, when Descartes doubts he has a body, the doubt is not a property of his body; it is merely a psychological attitude toward it. To appreciate the problem more clearly, consider the following argument with the same form.

> Tim does not doubt that Ralph Lauren is a famous clothing designer.
> Tim does doubt that Ralph Lifshitz is a famous clothing designer.
> Therefore, Ralph Lauren is not identical to Ralph Lifshitz.

The fact of the matter is that Ralph Lauren *is* Ralph Lifshitz (he changed his name), so even though the premises are true (Tim does not know Lauren changed his name from Lifshitz), the argument must be invalid. The source of the problem must be that the doubting (or not doubting) is a state of Tim's mind and not a property of Ralph Lauren or of Ralph Lifshitz. Since the argument does not identify genuine properties, it cannot employ Leibniz's Law to distinguish Lauren from Lifshitz. This argument is therefore guilty of an error often called the **intensional fallacy**. Descartes's argument is guilty of this fallacy too because it also treats doubt as though it were a property of the thing doubted. In both arguments it is more appropriate to treat doubt as an activity of the person doing the doubting. The fact that Descartes can doubt the existence of his mind but not of his body does not prove therefore that mind and body are distinct substances, for he has not shown that mind and body possess different properties.

Descartes's second argument for dualism occurs much later in the *Meditations*. At this point the epistemological project is complete. Descartes believes he knows that God exists and that God has given him the ability to distinguish between truth and falsity. In *Meditation Six* he offers the following alternative argument for a distinction between mind and body.

> My body is divisible.
> My mind is indivisible.
> Therefore, my mind is not identical to my body.

In this argument Descartes identifies **genuine properties**. Divisibility and indivisibility are not psychological attitudes toward things but are characteristics of things themselves. This argument therefore does not commit the error we saw in Descartes's previous use of Leibniz's Law. Descartes believes the first premise is true because, in his view, divisibility is an essential property of material bodies. That is, part of what it means for something to be a physical thing is that it is divisible, for all physical things can decay, which is the breaking down of a body into its parts. He also thinks there is good reason to accept the second premise because he simply cannot conceive of the possibility of dividing the mind into parts. Although the mind is divisible in a sense, this involves a different meaning of the word "divisible" than the one used in the first premise of the argument. When Descartes talks about the different kinds of mental operations of which the mind is capable (sensing, understanding, doubting, etc.), one might think he is saying that the mind is also divisible. To divide the mind in this sense is completely different from dividing matter into its parts. Distinguishing between doubting and understanding is a method of **categorizing** mental operations or faculties; it is not

taking mental states and splitting them up into simpler compo-
nents as we do when we divide matter. When we divide a material object into its constituent parts, we get smaller material
bodies. However, when we divide the mind into its various
faculties, we do not get smaller minds. Thus, Descartes has
persuasive reasons for accepting these premises. Since the argument identifies genuine properties, it uses Leibniz's Law properly, and so the conclusion follows from the premises.

Critics of this argument usually suggest that although the
conclusion follows from the premises, it does so only because
the argument **begs the question**. When an argument begs the
question, it assumes the truth of the conclusion somewhere in
the premises. Since premises are supposed to *establish* a
conclusion (not *assume* its truth), this is a bad form of argument; it is arguing in a circle. Those who disagree with
Descartes's second argument claim that the flaw lies in the
second premise: *My mind is indivisible.* To claim that the mind
is indivisible is already to assume it is non-physical, yet the
point of the argument is to show that mind and body are
distinct kinds of substances. Just because Descartes cannot
conceive of his mind being divided into parts does not mean
that it cannot be so divided. If his mind were a physical thing
(whether he realizes it or not), then it could be divided into
parts just like any other material object.

For now, let's assume Descartes's arguments for dualism are
compelling. Because Descartes's theory claims that human
beings are a composite of two substances (mind and body), this
view is often called **substance dualism**. Descartes treats the body
as a physical substance the essential nature of which is extension
(three-dimensionality) and the workings of which can be

explained primarily in terms of the mathematical principles of the new scientific physics. The mind, on the other hand, is essentially a conscious thinking thing and is the ultimate source of one's personal identity. To treat mind and body as distinct substances raises obvious questions about how they are connected. Descartes observes that although he is composed of both a mental substance and a physical substance, the two are so intimately connected that together they make up one thing. However, he also claims that since the mind or soul is unextended and indivisible, it cannot decay like the body and so will likely survive the death of the body as a disembodied soul. If mind and body are two such radically different kinds of things or substances, we should wonder how exactly they are connected.

The Problem of Interaction

In the *Meditations* Descartes proposes that there is a *causal interaction* between mind and body. This view is called **interactionism**. What reasons are there to think that mind and body causally interact? Assuming dualism is true, we have all kinds of evidence of a causal interaction between mind and body. When I realize I am thirsty, I form the intention in my mind to stand up and get myself a drink. I then stand up, walk to the kitchen, and open the refrigerator. I see a bottle of beer on one of the shelves and grab it. Here we have several different kinds of causal interactions between mind and body. Light waves reflected from the surface of the bottle of beer stimulate my retinas and cause the sensation of a bottle of beer in my mind.

The intentions I formulate in my mind, both to get a drink and to grab the beer, cause bodily actions by which I accomplish both these things. Thus, it seems perfectly obvious that mind and body interact.

While it seems that there is causal interaction between mind and body, it is difficult to understand *how* this happens. We require an explanation of how non-physical minds causally interact with physical bodies. Descartes gestures at an explanation in the *Meditations* but provides a considerably more detailed account of mind-body interaction in his last philosophical work *Passions of the Soul*. Descartes was not a mere armchair philosopher but also dissected a lot of brains and bodies and thus knew a great deal about physiology. Playing a central role in his account of the mind-body relation is the *pineal gland* or *conarion*, a small gland located roughly in the centre of the brain. In Descartes's time its function was unknown. Because the physiology then claimed that sensory information traveled along two tracks in the brain, the central location of the pineal gland made it a good candidate to serve as the place where the interaction between mind and body occurred, for it could act as a kind of funnel that would unite the flow of information to a central point.

Let's use the example of my deciding to get up and then doing so to illustrate the basic principles of Descartes's theory. According to Descartes, what happens is that I form the intention to get up in my mind or soul and this causes a motion of the pineal gland in the brain. The movement of the pineal gland causes the flow of a fluid that exists throughout the body called the **animal spirits**. The animal spirits flow to the muscles which cause them to contract and expand in such a way that I stand up and go to the kitchen as I intended. The same principles explain how the body affects the mind. When the light waves reflected off the surface of the bottle of beer stimulate the retinas in my eyes, this stimulation causes a motion of the animal spirits. The spirits travel to my brain and cause another motion of the pineal gland. This time the pineal gland stimulates my soul so as to produce the sensation of a bottle of beer in my mind.

This account is somewhat oversimplified, but it does show that Descartes has a fairly detailed story to tell about how mind and body interact. With recent advances in physiology and neuroscience there are, of course, reasons to be sceptical about most of these details. For instance, physiologists have shown there is no such thing as the animal spirits and have found that the pineal gland is part of the hormonal system. A charitable interpretation of these discoveries is to say that although he gets the details wrong, Descartes may have been on the right track. One might think that the animal spirits are really just a clumsy seventeenth-century understanding of the electrochemical impulses of the central nervous system. Furthermore, we know the brain is extremely important for explaining thought, perception, and intentional actions, so even if he is wrong about the pineal gland, perhaps Descartes is correct that the brain (or some other part of it) acts as the transducer between mind and body. While this is charitable indeed, vague talk about the brain is hardly satisfactory. It is one thing to say that the pineal gland (or some other part of the brain) causes things to happen in the mind (and vice versa), but it is another to explain how the interaction occurs.

There are two ways to interpret the nature of this problem. The first is a matter of confessing ignorance and insisting that

Descartes has not yet explained how the interaction happens. In this case, we are simply asking for a deeper account that includes the details about how brain and soul enter into causal relationships. To say that the motion of the pineal gland (or any other part of the brain) causes the occurrence of ideas in the soul is only to state *that* these two things interact; it does not *explain how*. Thus, critics of Cartesian dualism often say the theory is unacceptable because it is too mysterious; it leaves too much unexplained.

A dualist could reply to this objection by saying that the demand to explain how mind and body causally interact is unreasonable because we don't yet possess a deep understanding of causation in general, even of causal relations between physical things. If causality is itself a mystery and we can't explain the details of how one physical thing causes another, then why should Descartes have to explain the details of mind-body causation? Such a demand seems excessive unless those who make it can say with confidence that we understand all the details of causal relations between physical things. It is unlikely anybody would claim they do, in which case the first interpretation of the problem with interactionism is not entirely convincing. However, Descartes's critics could respond to this objection by saying that it underestimates how much we know about causal relationships between physical things. Our success in building technology and in developing things like vaccines surely shows that we understand *something* about cause and effect. While there might be some unresolved *philosophical* issues about the nature of causation, causal relationships between physical things do not seem very mysterious, for we understand how a vaccine causes immunity to a disease and we understand how stepping on the brake pedal in a car causes the vehicle to slow down. The same, it seems, is not true of causal relationships between minds and bodies, and thus the problem remains.

The second interpretation of the problem goes beyond claiming it is a mystery how mind and body interact; it claims such an idea is incoherent. Imagine that we could examine my getting up to get a beer in fantastic detail. We can explain the movement of my body by appealing to the expansion and contraction of certain muscles, and we can explain why those muscles expand and contract by identifying certain electro-chemical impulses sent from the brain. Is there any reason to think that if we could trace the causal origins of my getting up far enough back into the brain that we will discover a point at which we will observe a non-physical soul exerting causal influence on a state of the brain? If interactionism is true, there must be such a point. Because the brain and all its parts are located in space, there must be some place in the brain where the interaction between mind and body occurs—a **locus of interaction**. Descartes tells us, however, that the mind is non-physical and so does not occupy space. If the mind cannot occupy space, then there can be no place in the brain or point of space where the interaction happens. This is what gives rise to the charge of incoherence. The problem is that interactionism requires a locus of interaction, but the non-physical nature of mental substance precludes the possibility of there being such a locus of interaction. Thus, interactionism seems incoherent.

These kinds of concerns have proven devastating to interactionism. Most philosophers agree that the problem of interaction is a serious blow to Cartesian dualism. Historically, the first reaction to this problem was to adopt Descartes's dualism but reject his claim that mind and body interact. This gave rise to the forms of **parallelism** described below.

Parallelism

Some philosophers were convinced that the physical world is a closed system of causes and effects between physical bodies and forces. They also thought Descartes was correct that we have both physical bodies and non-physical minds. Since these philosophers believed that a causal interaction between mind and body is incoherent, they simply denied that any interaction occurs. In their view the body—being a part of the physical world—acts as it does solely because of its place within a network of causal relationships with other material bodies. Non-physical states such as thoughts, decisions, and desires can have no causal influence on the body.

This seems very counterintuitive. As we saw in our discussion of interactionism, our everyday experiences strongly suggest that mind and body interact. It seems simply obvious that the stimulation of my retinas by that bottle of beer causes me to have a certain kind of sensation. It also seems obvious that mental states like decisions sometimes cause our bodies to do things, as when I decide to get up for a drink. Some philosophers admit that things seem this way, but claim that in light of the problem of interaction the way things seem is misleading. Their task, then, is to explain why it seems as if there is a causal connection between mind and body when there is not.

The explanation for these apparent (but unreal) causal

interactions is that mind and body operate in parallel. There is no causal interaction between the two, but they travel along parallel courses that make it seem as though the two interact. This view is called *parallelism.* Advocates of this view (*parallelists*) offer a very different account of what happens when I see that bottle of beer in the refrigerator. While interactionists would say that the stimulation of my retinas causes, via the pineal gland, the sensation of a bottle of beer in my mind, parallelists would say that the stimulation of my retinas only produces other physical events. Nothing in the physical world causes me to have that sensation. It just so happens that my mind has the sensation of a bottle of beer when my body is looking at one. Similarly, if someone drops a rock on my head, I experience a corresponding sensation of pain, but the pain is not caused by the impact of the rock on my head or by any subsequent physiological processes. Because our sensations are always correlated with certain bodily events, it seems as if the bodily events cause the sensations, but this is not so.

How is it that the mind always has sensations that are appropriate to the condition of the body? What principle explains why mind and body always function in parallel? The parallelists appealed to God to explain the source of mind-body parallelism. Gottfried Wilhelm von Leibniz and Nicholas Malebranche, the best-known advocates of parallelism, gave God slightly different roles in their explanations. Leibniz claimed that when God created the universe, He did it in a way that would ensure mind and body would always run along parallel courses. Thus, the parallelism was set up by God from the very beginning. This view is called **pre-established harmony**. Malebranche, on the other hand, claimed that God intervenes whenever necessary to cause minds to have the appropriate sensations. This view is called **occasionalism** since God must produce a sensation on every occasion that the sensory organs of the body are properly stimulated. To contrast these two accounts further, let's return to the example of my seeing the beer in my refrigerator. Leibniz would say that it was predetermined by God at the moment of creation both that I would have the sensation of a bottle of beer at that very moment in time and that my eyes would be looking at a bottle of beer at that moment. The sensation is not caused by the beer, but by God's creative act. Malbranche agrees with the claim that the sensation is caused by God, but doesn't think God caused me to have it by virtue of the way God created the universe. Instead, Malbranche believes that God caused my mind to have this sensation at the precise moment when my eyes fixed on that bottle of beer.

Although parallelism sounds very implausible at first, we can see that Leibniz and Malebranche formulated it in a way that renders it consistent with our experiences. Their appeals to acts of God explain why it seems that mind and body causally interact when in fact they don't. Because the parallelists denied that there is any causal interaction between mind and body they escaped some of the difficulties that plagued Cartesian dualism, such as the problem of interaction. However, the parallelists had their own share of philosophical difficulties.

The first and most obvious problem is that parallelists accepted Descartes's reasons for adopting dualism, and, as we have already seen, those arguments are not very compelling. Second, philosophers attacked Leibniz's theory on the grounds that it is fatalistic. The pre-established harmony arranged by God seems to imply that we have no control over our minds or our bodies. We seem to be nothing more than complex wind-up toys whose every action was prearranged at the moment of creation. The third and most significant complaint against parallelism is that it is overly complex, both in its explanations of human experience and in its metaphysical commitments. To many philosophers the need to appeal to a divine being to explain why we have the sensations we do is unattractive when much simpler explanations are possible. Although interactionism is mysterious, one might argue that it is preferable to having to rely on God to explain the origin of our sensations. To rely on God as the parallelists did we would require philosophical reasons to believe in God's existence. Furthermore, it is surely just as mysterious, if not more so, to explain how God causes our sensations as to explain how our bodies do. In light of these kinds of considerations, parallelism has not been a very popular theory.

Epiphenomenalism

A second, more recent response to interactionism is a view called **epiphenomenalism**. T.H. Huxley is usually credited with originating this theory in the late 1800s. Like the parallelists, the epiphenomenalists could not see a way to make sense of the idea that non-physical events, such as choices or decisions, could influence matter. Thus, epiphenomenalists shared with Leibniz and Malebranche the claim that mental states cannot cause physical happenings. However, they differed from the parallelists because they thought mental events, states, or processes are the effects of neurological states. In their view, the brain has the power to produce non-physical states. The causal relationship between mind and brain is therefore a one-way relationship. Brain states can cause mental states, but mental states cannot cause brain states. According to epiphenomenalism, mental states are a special kind of causal by-product of events in the brain.

Because epiphenomenalists deny that our mental states have physical effects they need to explain why it *seems* as though our mental states sometimes cause bodily behaviour. My decision to get up, which is a non-physical mental event, seems to cause my getting up, which is a physical, bodily event. What is going on here according to the epiphenomenalist? A myriad of physical processes in my body produce a certain neural event. This neural event causes the mental event that is my deciding to get up. In addition to causing my deciding to get up, the neural event also causes other neural events that have effects on my muscles. These other neural events eventually cause my getting up. Thus, my bodily behaviour has causal origins that are completely physical, but because one link in that causal chain also produces my decision, it seems as if my decision caused my behaviour. This is simply an illusion resulting from the fact that my decisions precede my actions.

Epiphenomenalism is an attractive view to some because it gives causal priority to physical events and thus treats the physical realm as a closed, causal system. It is also attractive because it claims that mental states depend completely on the brain and there is a great deal of evidence to suggest that there is an intimate connection between mind and brain. However, epiphenomenalism faces some serious philosophical obstacles. First, although it is consistent with our experience, many find this view unappealing because it dismisses agency as an illusion. If epiphe-nomenalism is true, we never act for reasons or because we decide to; our having reasons and making decisions are just causally powerless by-products of our neural states. If one is tempted to think that our mental states really do cause our behaviour (as seems to be the case), then this position does not hold much appeal. Of course, wanting to believe in genuine agency is not a good reason for rejecting epiphenomenalism, for it could be that there is no agency in this sense, in which case the epiphenomenalists need only explain the mechanisms that generate the *appearance of agency*, which they have already done.

A more successful challenge to epiphenomenalism focuses on the claim that neural events can cause non-physical states. Recall that epiphenomenalism is, at least in part, motivated by the problems of interactionism. That is, epiphenomenalists thought it inconceivable that mental states could have causal influence on physical states. If they took this problem so seri-ously, it is hard to see how they could claim that neural states can produce mental ones while remaining consistent. To accept the principle of one-way causation between brain and mind is still to accept the idea that there is *some* causal interaction between mind and body. One-way causation is a causal rela-tionship, and how the physical processes of the brain could cause non-physical states is a complete mystery. Thus, epiphe-nomenalism does not really appear to be a significant improvement over Cartesian dualism.

Conclusion

In this chapter we have seen several different forms of dualism. Although there are philosophers who currently advocate some form of dualism, the general consensus is that dualism is very implausible. The main problem with it is, as we saw, that once the human subject is divided into two parts with radically different natures, it is extremely difficult to explain how these parts are related in a way that is philosophically defensible. For this reason, most philosophers of mind have turned away from dualism toward some form of materialism. By claiming that human beings are wholly physical, and that mental states are nothing more than complex physical states, the problem of interaction is circumvented altogether. As we shall see, however, there are a number of competing forms of materialism, each of which faces its own philosophical problems.

Suggestions for Further Reading

Descartes, R. 1988. *Descartes: Selected Philosophical Writings*. Cambridge; New York: Cambridge University Press.

Huxley, T.H. 1896. "On the Hypothesis That Animals Are Automata, and Its History." *Methods and Results: Essays*. New York: D. Appleton and Co.

Leibniz, G.W., ed. 1988. *Monadology, and Other Philosophical Essays*. Library of Liberal Arts. New York: Macmillan.

CHAPTER 2

■ BEHAVIOURISM

Historical Context

The theory of mind we will discuss in this chapter arose in the wake of a broader philosophical movement known as **logical positivism**, which reached the height of its popularity in the 1940s and 1950s. The positivists adopted a rigorous commitment to empiricism; many of them believed all knowledge and inquiry should have its foundations in matters that are publicly observable. Many philosophers adopted positivism as a means of escaping from the traditional metaphysical questions that have resisted resolution by showing that issues like the mind-body problem should not be solved, but *dissolved*. This involved a therapeutic approach to philosophy, which claimed that we should not have taken most philosophical problems seriously in the first place. The general idea was that many such problems are the result of linguistic and logical confusion and that once these confusions are revealed we will see that the problems are illusory.

The aim of such philosophers was to map out the logic of our ordinary concepts and to show that a proper understanding of this logic helps us avoid most philosophical problems.

Behaviourists like Gilbert Ryle adopted this kind of approach to the mind-body problem. In his influential book *The Concept of Mind*, Ryle argues that the kinds of considerations that motivate dualism and create the mind-body problem in the first place are the result of various linguistic and logical errors that he calls **category mistakes**. By identifying these various category mistakes and clarifying the logic of our psychological concepts, Ryle claims to show that the mind-body problem is an illusion. In his view, there is no problem of how mind and body are related because there is no such thing as a mind in the Cartesian sense. Although he was not himself a positivist, Ryle's account of the logic of our concepts was strongly influenced by the positivist theory of meaning called **verificationism**. According to this theory, the meaning of a sentence must be understood in relation to the observable conditions that verify or falsify the claim. If a sentence cannot be verified or falsified empirically, then the sentence is meaningless. This does not mean that each and every sentence has to be verified or falsified in practice. The claim "Fran is at the office" is meaningful even if no one goes to the office and checks. What matters is that there is some way *in principle* to verify or falsify the claim empirically. That is, we know what the claim "Fran is at the office" means because we know how to verify or falsify the claim, even if we never bother to do so in practice.

The identified target of Ryle's attack in *The Concept of Mind* is what he calls **the official doctrine**: the common sense understanding of human beings as embodied minds—an understanding that is essentially Cartesian. At its heart is a polar opposition between minds and bodies. Conventional wisdom tells us that we have bodies that occupy space and that are material objects that obey the laws of nature and, as such, can be the objects of scientific study. In principle there is nothing mysterious about our bodies. We might not completely understand how the body functions, but this is not because there are parts of the body that are immune to scientific scrutiny; the limits on our understanding are due entirely to the complexity of the body (especially the brain) and the relative novelty of our scientific theories (such as neurology).

Our minds, on the other hand, seem quite mysterious. A surgeon can open my skull and study my brain with a variety of instruments, but my mind seems to be something essentially private. I know directly through introspection what my thoughts are. I know what I feel, desire, and think. For instance, I don't need to guess whether or not I believe it is going to rain today; I just know I believe it. When it comes to knowing what another person's mental states are, the situation is quite different. We do not simply observe what others believe. Usually we rely on what they say and how they act to determine what they think. For example, if you wanted to know whether or not I think it is going to rain today, you might watch to see if I take my umbrella with me when I go outside. Alternatively, you might take a more direct approach and ask me "Do you think it is going to rain today?" and then use my response "Yes" to determine what I think. Either way, you will need to draw inferences about what I believe, and there is always the possibility that those inferences might be mistaken. Perhaps I want to take my umbrella to my office and leave it there in case of rainy days in the distant future, and perhaps I thought you asked me "Do you think Ike's going to Spain today?" These kinds of considerations tend to make us think that the mind is private in a way the body is not.

When you try to find out whether or not I believe it is going to rain today, you make an assumption that is central to the official doctrine: that my mental states (in this case my belief that it is going to rain today) are causes of my behaviour. That is, in order to consider my umbrella carrying and my utterance as evidence of what I believe, you must think that what I believe *caused* my behaviour. If my actions didn't have anything to do with what I believe, then you couldn't use the former as evidence for claims about the latter. According to the official doctrine, then, mental states are *hidden inner causes of behaviour.* Ryle refers to this as the dogma of **the ghost in the machine**. This is because when we think about ourselves in the way described here, we treat the mind like a ghostly entity that occupies the body and the body as a complex machine whose workings are occasionally governed by mysterious mental causes. This is essentially Descartes's view, and so Ryle's attack on this idea is instructive for learning about other philosophical attacks on Cartesian dualism.

The Behavioural Analysis of Mental States

Ryle rejects the idea that mental states are ghostly inner causes of behaviour for two related reasons. The first has to do with epistemic implications of the official doctrine. According to Ryle, the Cartesian view leads to the absurd conclusion that we can't know the minds of others or, indeed, whether or not other people have minds at all. We will examine this complaint below. Ryle's second reason is connected with his commitment to empiricism. If we treat mental states as essentially private inner states, there is no way for us to have empirical evidence of what someone else thinks or feels. While it is true that the official doctrine claims we can (and frequently do) appeal to behavioural evidence to draw conclusions about the minds of others, this is not satisfactory. All this accomplishes is the justification of claims about behaviour itself, not about its inner causes. Since the official doctrine treats mental states as *essentially* private, there is in principle no way to know what those states are empirically.

In light of these problems, Ryle offers an alternative account of what we are doing when we make claims about the minds of others. In his view, when we attribute a mental state to someone, we are not identifying the inner causes of their behaviour; instead, we are really talking about the behaviour itself. Because behaviour is publicly observable, this gives us empirical means to evaluate sentences about what others think and feel and thus allows us to have knowledge about the minds of others.

Central to the behaviourist understanding of mental states is the concept of a **disposition**, a tendency to act in certain ways under certain circumstances. We often understand chemical properties of substances as dispositions. For example, to say that a sugar cube is water soluble is to say how it would behave if it were immersed in unsaturated water—it would dissolve. Although we say that a sugar cube *is* water soluble, solubility is not an inner state of the sugar cube, and it is certainly not an inner cause of its dissolving; it is only a claim about how it would behave under a specific set of circumstances. According to behaviourists, when we claim that an individual believes or feels such and such, we are not talking about the causes of their behaviour either; we are really identifying a set of dispositions. The kinds of dispositions human beings are capable of are much more complicated than the dispositions of a sugar cube. We understand solubility in terms of a single disposition. By comparison, mental states involve reference to a vast array of dispositions.

Let's return to the example in which it is true that I believe it is going to rain today. The official doctrine treats this belief as the cause of (among other things) my carrying my umbrella and of my saying "Yes" when asked "Do you believe it is going to rain today?" By contrast, the behaviourist claims my believing that it is going to rain today consists of nothing more than a complex set of dispositions. To believe it is going to rain *just is* to be disposed to carry one's umbrella, not to wear suede shoes, to respond with the utterance "Yes" when asked "Do you believe it is going to rain today," and so on. Because this understanding of my mental state in terms of a set of dispositions is explained by making reference to publicly observable behaviour, this view is called **behaviourism**. Behaviourists believe we can analyze all mental states in terms of behavioural dispositions, which is why this view is sometimes called **analytical behaviourism**.

The paragraph above provides a behavioural analysis of a belief. What do behaviourists say about sensations like pain? They say that pain is something we should also understand as a set of dispositions. Suppose I hit my thumb with a hammer. Doing so results in certain typical kinds of behaviour: yelling, cursing, nursing the injured thumb, and so on. The official doctrine claims that these are caused by a private sensation that was itself caused by smashing my thumb with a hammer. Since behaviourists want to eliminate any reference to such hidden causes, they claim that my being in pain *just is* being disposed to yell, curse, and nurse my thumb.

The Category Mistake

Ryle believes the behaviourist analysis of mental states reflects the logic of our psychological concepts more accurately than the official doctrine because, as we just saw, the criteria on the grounds of which we attribute mental states to others are purely behavioural. Ryle's alternative understanding of this logic leads him to claim that the official doctrine is guilty of what he calls a **category mistake**. This is a difficult concept that Ryle tries to clarify by using a number of examples. Let's consider one of these and then try to draw out the nature of the problem.

Suppose one day a friend from out of town visits you in order to see the university you attend, so you take her on a tour of the campus. You show her the arts building, the science building, the library, the athletic complex, the student centre where you eat lunch, and so on. Now suppose that at the end of the tour your friend looks at you somewhat impatiently and says, "You've shown me the arts building, the science building, the library, the athletic complex, and the student centre—which are all lovely—but where is the university?" Such a remark should seem strange, and you would rightly think your friend is confused. What has gone wrong? By insisting that she has not seen the university, although she has seen all the buildings on the campus, your friend has failed to realize that the university *just is* the collection of buildings (and their institutional relations) and not something else in addition to them. She probably expected the university to be something else, perhaps something like the arts building but different. Your friend has made a category mistake.

To understand the precise nature of the confusion, we need to understand the concept of a category. A category is a class or group made up of individual members that share a particular characteristic. For example, *animal* is a category whose membership consists of cats, rats, elephants, and so on. Anything and everything that is an animal is a member of this class or category. When someone makes a category mistake, they falsely think that something from one category is a member of another category. To return to our example, when your friend denies having seen the university, she mistakenly thought that a university belongs to the category of *concrete things*, of which the arts building, the library, and so on, are all members. Since a university is not itself a concrete thing like a building, it does not belong to the same category as the buildings seen on the tour.

You might wonder why your friend would make such a silly mistake. According to Ryle, category mistakes are quite common. In most cases, we make them because of features of our language. Words that refer to quite different kinds of things often play similar grammatical roles in sentences, and it is these similar roles that make us think of the things to which these words refer as things of the same kind. For example, on several occasions you might have said to your friend "I am going to the library" and you might also have said "I am going to the university." Because the university and the library play similar roles in these two sentences, one might think that the word "library" denotes something from the same category as what is denoted by "university." This of course is not true, which becomes apparent when one points out that it makes sense to ask which floor of the library you are going to, but it does not make sense to ask which floor of the university you will be visiting. Now that we know what a category mistake is, how does the official doctrine make one?

According to Ryle, the official doctrine makes a category mistake by assuming that the mind is something over and above the bodily behaviour we observe in others. That is, just as it was a mistake for your friend to think that the university was something *in addition to* the buildings on the campus (and their institutional affiliations), it is a mistake to think that the mind is something in addition to behaviour. As we saw, Ryle believes category mistakes are the result of features of our language. The source of the error in the traditional doctrine is that we often speak about mental states in the same way that we talk about the physiological processes that cause our bodily movement. For example, on the one hand we say things like "My hand went up *because* my muscles contracted," and on the other we say things like "My hand went up *because* I decided to raise it." The second claim treats my deciding as though it belonged to the same category of things, events, or processes, as the contraction of my muscles in the first claim. However, since my deciding to do something is, according to the traditional doctrine, unobservable, it must be a ghostly, non-physical event or process.

Once we recognise this and other similar category mistakes

and adopt Ryle's alternative account of the logic of our psychological concepts, we can do away with the idea that there are non-physical causes of our behaviour that are housed in an immaterial soul. When we abandon our belief in non-physical minds there is no longer any need to connect the mind to the body by appealing to a mysterious metaphysical principle, so the mind-body problem simply dissolves. For if the mind is merely a collection of dispositions, and we should understand dispositions in terms of bodily behaviour, the question about how mind and body interact does not arise. On the behaviourist view, human beings are just complex physical bodies.

The Problem of Other Minds

Ryle's other complaint against the official doctrine is that it leads us to a philosophical absurdity, which takes the following form. The official doctrine has the implication that we can never really know the contents of the minds of others, yet we have every reason to believe that we do possess such knowledge. For instance, you normally feel confident that you know your mother loves you, that your friends feel pain when they injure themselves, and so on. If the official doctrine leads us to the conclusion that we cannot know such things, then something is probably wrong with the official doctrine. The concern that we might not know what other people think and feel is called **the problem of other minds**. In Ryle's view, since the official doctrine gives rise to the problem of other minds, we would be better off abandoning the official doctrine.

How does the official doctrine give rise to the problem of other minds? Since the official doctrine tells us that mental states are private, inner causes of behaviour to which we have privileged access through introspection, it follows that we can only learn about the mental states of others *indirectly*. To return to an earlier example, since you cannot simply observe my belief that it is going to rain (because it is private), you need to rely on my behaviour and use it as evidence to draw inferences about what I believe. Thus, you listen to what I have to say, observe what I do, and then try to draw a conclusion about what I think. As we saw, this can be tricky, for the evidence is subject to a variety of interpretations and can therefore be misleading. For instance, I could have many different reasons for carrying my umbrella.

The most popular philosophical response to the problem of other minds has been to employ an analogy between oneself and others to justify inferences about their mental states. This is called the **argument from analogy**. John Stuart Mill formulated the argument along the following lines. I know that I have a body and that I have a mind. I also know when I feel pain, and under what conditions this happens. That is, I know in my own case that a sensation of pain has certain kinds of causes and effects. It is caused by bodily injury (such as hitting one's thumb with a hammer), and the pain in turn produces certain kinds of reactions: I grasp my thumb, yell and curse, and so on. Furthermore, I know in my own case that the pain is necessary for the resulting behaviour to occur under these circumstances. That is, if I hit my thumb with a hammer but it doesn't hurt, then I don't yell or exhibit other kinds of pain-behaviour. When it comes to other people, although I can't observe their pains, I can observe the same kinds of causes and effects at work in their behaviour. I can witness them hit their thumbs with hammers, and I can see that this is followed by the same kind of pain-behaviour I exhibit when I hit my thumb with a hammer: I see them grasp their thumbs, swear, and so on. The question is whether or not the same sensation (pain) mediates between these causes and effects in their cases as in mine. Since I know the sensation *has to happen* in my case, since it is necessary for the pain-behaviour, and since I know that other humans are physically very similar to me, I am justified in believing that the sensation is necessary for others as well. Thus, I can conclude that other people feel pain under conditions sufficiently similar to the conditions under which I feel pain. I can extend this line of reasoning to all kinds of thoughts and sensations, in which case I can have knowledge of other people's minds.

Many philosophers have attacked this style of argument on the grounds that using one's own case to draw conclusions about the minds of others is insufficient to justify the inference that others feel pain. The complaint is that one's own experiences are too small a sample to build upon in order to support inferences about everyone else. Let's use another example to help illustrate the point. Suppose you have noticed that whenever you drink beer you belch, and that this happens with every kind of beer you have ever consumed. You might want to draw the conclusion that all beer makes you belch. To do this is to draw a kind of **inductive inference.** You are formulating a conclusion about a whole bunch of things you haven't yet experienced on the basis of experiences you have had in the past. Your experiences of drinking beer and belching constitute what is called a *sample,* and the group of things you want to draw a conclusion about is called the *population*. The strength of your inference is directly proportional to the size of the sample; the larger your sample, the more reliable your inference. The more times you have consumed beer with the same result (belching), and the more varieties of beer you have tried, the more probable it is that your conclusion is true. If you have only had one glass of beer your entire life, then your conclusion is obviously less certain, for perhaps there was something special about that particular glass of beer that is different from most others, or perhaps there was something special about the circumstances under which you drank it. Increasing the number of experienced cases in the sample lowers the likelihood of such possibilities and increases the probability of the conclusion.

The complaint against the argument from analogy is that using one's own experiences of pain to conclude that others feel pain under relevantly similar conditions is like arguing that all beer makes you belch on the basis of a single experience. If you knew that 1,000 people feel pain under certain conditions, then you could more reliably conclude that all people feel pain under those conditions, but this is not the case. All you know about are *your own* pains, so your sample is limited to one person. Even though you may have a lifetime of experience, and have been in pain thousands of times, you are still only a sample of one, and that is too small a sample to support an inference about billions of other people.

Stuart Hampshire has offered a clever way to improve the argument from analogy. While it is true that a sample of one is normally too small to draw inductive inferences, he argues that if we can find a way to show that the *inference* in the argument from analogy is reliable, the fact that the sample is so small won't be a serious concern. The goal, then, is to find reasons for thinking that the general pattern of argument in the argument from analogy is a good one that gives us true conclusions. Once we have such reasons, we can employ the argument from analogy to draw conclusions about the minds of others, even from one's own limited case. The trick is to observe other people using the argument from analogy to draw inferences about *your* mental states. Since you have access to the contents of your mind, you are in the unique position of being able to tell whether or not those inferences are correct. Imagine that one day your friend sees you hit your thumb with a hammer, and she says correctly "You must be in pain." You ask her how she arrived at this conclusion and she offers the following explanation:

> Whenever I hit my thumb with a hammer, I've noticed that it causes in me a sensation of pain, which in turn causes certain kinds of behaviour. I've realized that the sensation is necessary for the behaviour because I don't act that way when I hit my thumb but don't feel pain. Because I know you have a body that is relevantly similar to mine, I argued using an analogy between my cases to yours. You just smashed your thumb with a hammer and exhibited pain-behaviour, so I concluded that you must be in pain.

Once enough people have run through this line of reasoning enough times, you have every reason to believe the pattern of argument is a reliable one, for you have seen it yield true conclusions about the states of your mind over and over again. You now have reason to believe the argument from analogy is a good argument. In light of this, you are free to employ it to draw conclusions about the minds of others, in which case the problem of other minds is no longer an insurmountable one.

Although Hampshire's proposal is quite ingenious, it is unfortunately unsuccessful at vindicating the argument from analogy. As Norman Malcolm has pointed out, Hampshire's approach *begs the question*. To say an argument begs the question means that it assumes the truth of the conclusion it is supposed to establish. Here's the problem. In order to learn that the argument from analogy is a reliable argument, I need to see other people use it successfully; other people have to use it to draw correct inferences about my mental states. For this to happen, I need to make certain assumptions. First, I need to assume that other people observe my behaviour and draw inferences. Second, I need to assume that they are using their access to their own mental states in the process of drawing inferences about what I think and feel. If I don't make these assumptions, then it is hard to see how I could interpret other people as using the argument from analogy in the first place. Once we appreciate the nature of these assumptions, the problem with Hampshire's approach becomes clear. All of these assumptions presuppose that other people have minds. *Observing* my behaviour, *drawing inferences, accessing their own mental states* are all activities that require the claim that other people have minds. This, of course, is precisely the point of contention. The whole reason for wanting to show that the argument from analogy is a reliable argument is that we don't really know whether or not other people have minds. Hampshire simply assumes that they do in his defence of the argument from analogy, so he begs the question.

Few philosophers believe that the argument from analogy

can be improved sufficiently to solve the problem of other minds. Even if we could use a method like Hampshire's without begging the question, the strongest conclusion an inductive inference can get us is one to the effect that other people *probably* have minds like our own. This is because probable conclusions are the best that *any* inductive argument can get us. All inductive arguments rely on experienced cases (the sample) and our experience is always limited, so such arguments can never give us absolutely certain conclusions. The only way I could be absolutely sure that all beer makes me belch would be if I made the sample equal to the population, that is, if I drank all the beer that there is (or will be), but then I would not need to draw an inference to know whether the conclusion is true or false. It is clearly impossible to extend the sample in the argument from analogy beyond my own experiences to include the minds of others in the way I can extend the sample of beer consumed by drinking more. For all these reasons, the argument from analogy does not look like a very promising solution to the problem of other minds.

Ryle agrees that the problem of other minds is an intractable one for reasons like the ones discussed above. When we are faced with a problem that we cannot solve, it is often a good idea to look at the considerations that gave rise to the problem in the first place. The problem of other minds became a problem only because we assumed the truth of the official doctrine—the idea that mental states are private, inner causes of behaviour. If we reject the official doctrine, then the problem of other minds disappears. This is yet another reason Ryle offers for adopting behaviourism and abandoning Cartesianism.

Problems with Behaviourism

Philosophers have identified two main problems with behaviourism. The first concerns the behaviourist account of sensations like pain. While it is true that being in pain is partly a matter of behaving a certain way, there is surely more to pain than this. There is also the way pain feels from the perspective of the person experiencing it. Pain has a certain qualitative character that is all too apparent when one is unfortunate enough to feel it. While it is true that you may curse and exhibit all kinds of pain-behaviour after a serious bodily injury, pain also *feels* a certain way to you, and this is not a matter of behaving this way or that. Furthermore, the way pain feels seems to be a private matter. Suppose an individual has been so fortunate that she has never felt pain. She can observe your pain-behaviour all she wants, and she can learn to use the word "pain" properly in English sentences, but that won't tell her what pain feels like. Since the behaviourist limits the account of what pain is to behavioural phenomena, he leaves out what is arguably pain's most important feature: *the way it feels*. This means the behaviourist's account of the nature of mental states is incomplete. Sensations must be more than dispositions to act in certain ways.

Behaviourists were sensitive to this problem. The most influential response to this kind of objection comes from Ludwig Wittgenstein, who argues that the commitment to the idea that there is a private, qualitative character common to all pains requires a **private language** and that such a language is absurd. Suppose for a moment that the above story were true: that being in pain is really just a matter of having a certain kind of private feeling. Since you can't access the way pain feels to others, and since they can't access the way pain feels to you, you can't rely on the public criteria we usually employ to determine when someone is in pain. For all we know, pain feels differently to other people than it does to you. You therefore need a new word to refer to this private feeling you have and to distinguish it from the public word "pain" that may or may not refer to the same feeling. Let's call it "pain*." So one day you have a sensation, which you identify as pain*, and several days later you have the same sensation again and say to yourself, "There's another pain*." The question is how you can be sure about this. How do you know that the feeling you have today is the same feeling you had several days ago? Maybe you no longer remember exactly what that feeling was like. Perhaps the feeling you have now is only similar to, but not the same as, the feeling you had before. The difficulty here is that without public criteria to determine the correct application of the word, you cannot tell whether or not you have used the word properly. If there is no way to be sure that you use the word "pain*" properly, you can't actually mean anything when you use it. According to Wittgenstein, this would be the plight of any private language. In light of this, we would be better off rejecting the idea that pain consists in the awareness of a certain kind of private experience.

While the first problem with behaviourism focused on mental states like sensations, the second takes aim at the behaviourist account of propositional attitudes such as beliefs. If the behaviourist is correct and mental states like beliefs are really just behavioural dispositions, then we should be able to abandon our psychological vocabulary and replace it without loss of meaning with a behavioural vocabulary. That is, if the behaviourist maintains that mental talk really is just a short-hand way of talking about behaviour, then we ought to be able to talk only about behaviour and still say everything we want to say using our mental vocabulary. The problem for the behaviourist is that this does not appear to be true.

Let's go back to our example of my believing it is going to rain today. According to the behaviourist, the claim that I believe it is going to rain today is really just a way of saying (among other things) that I am disposed to carry my umbrella, to wear a raincoat, not to wear suede shoes, and to respond affirmatively to questions like "Do you believe it is going to rain today?" For the behaviourist analysis to be complete, we need to talk only about these kinds of behavioural dispositions and avoid making any reference to other psychological states. If mental states creep back into the analysis, we are no longer providing a purely behavioural account of my belief. This is where the behaviourist gets into trouble.

First, let's consider the disposition Neil will respond by saying "Yes" if asked "Do you believe it is going to rain today?" While this disposition seems to capture part of what it is for me to have the belief in question, it does so only on certain assumptions. The behaviourist needs to assume that I understand English and so understood the question. She also needs to assume that I want to tell the truth and that by saying "Yes" I intended to answer the question. Now consider the disposition *Neil is disposed not to wear suede shoes.* The behaviourist has to work with some assumptions here too. For example, she has to assume that I like my shoes and don't want to ruin them. The thing to notice about these assumptions is that they all make reference to psychological states. *Understanding, want-*

ing, intending, and *liking* are all mental states that have not themselves been characterized as dispositions. The conclusion many philosophers draw from this kind of illustration is that no behavioural analysis of any mental state can ever appear plausible unless it makes assumptions of these kinds. That is, the only reason any analysis of a mental state in terms of dispositions seems adequate or plausible is because the analysis relies on implicit assumptions about other mental states in the background. The difficulty, then, is that the behaviourist is unable to provide an analysis of mental states that does not retain some mental residue. If behaviourism were true, it should be possible to provide an analysis without any mental residue. In this case, the behaviourist has failed to provide an analysis of the mental state solely in terms of dispositions, and so we once again have good reason to think that behaviourism provides an incomplete account of the nature of mental states.

Many philosophers regard this second objection as a decisive blow against behaviourism. Consequently, behaviourism is not a popular theory. As we will see later, however, other theories of mind that are popular today accept that the behaviourists captured something important in the connection they saw between mental states and behaviour. Current philosophers of mind just think the behaviourists were mistaken in their attempt to identify mental states *solely* with behavioural dispositions.

Suggestions for Further Reading

Hampshire, S. 1952. "The Analogy of Feeling." *Mind* 61: 1–12.

Malcolm, N. 1958. "Knowledge of Other Minds." *The Journal of Philosophy* 55: 969–78.

Ryle, G. 1963. *The Concept of Mind.* London: Hutchinson.

Wittgenstein, L. 1972. *Philosophical Investigations.* Trans. G.E.M. Anscombe. Oxford: Blackwell.

CHAPTER 3

■ TYPE IDENTITY THEORY

Consciousness as a Brain Process

Identity theorists, such as U.T. Place and J.J.C. Smart, claim that we should identify mental states with brain states. Place and Smart proposed the identity theory only for mental states like sensations, which they referred to generally as **consciousness**, because they believed that although behaviourism provided an adequate account of propositional attitudes like beliefs and desires, it was insufficient to account for qualitative states of consciousness such as feelings. Later identity theorists disagreed with behaviourism and adopted the identity theory for both sensations and propositional attitudes. This view is called **central state materialism**.

Because of his affiliation with behaviourism, Place is very careful to explain exactly what he means when he claims that consciousness is a brain state. He believes the claim that consciousness *is* a brain process is a very different kind of claim from the behaviourist's claim that a mental state *is* a behavioural state. Thus, he wants to be sure that his audience appreciates this fact. The difference between these two claims is not simply that one mentions brain states while the other talks about behaviour, although that is a difference. The important difference lies in the use of the word "is."

Place points out that we use the word "is" in several different ways. One of the most common uses is the "is" of **predication**. If I say "The ball *is* blue," I am merely saying that the ball has a certain property or characteristic, which is referred to linguistically as a *predicate*. Another use of the word "is" is the "is" of **composition**. When I say "A cloud *is* a collection of water droplets suspended in the atmosphere," I am not identifying a property of clouds but am telling you what clouds are made or composed of. The third use of the word "is" is the "is" of **definition**. If I say "A triangle *is* a three-sided planar figure whose internal angles add up to a sum of 180 degrees," I am using the word "is" differently again. I am not identifying the properties of a triangle, nor am I saying what triangles are made of; I am defining the word "triangle." Claims like the last one are often called **analytic** because they provide *an analysis of the meaning of the word.*

Recall from the previous chapter that, according to behaviourists, when we attribute a mental state to someone, this is really just a convenient way of talking about their behaviour. For example, to say "John feels pain" is just a handy way of saying that John is disposed to say "Ouch," to withdraw from the stimulus, and so on. The behaviourist analysis of our mental language in terms of dispositions is consequently a claim about what the words in our mental vocabulary really mean. Hence, the behaviourist's claim that a mental state *is* a behavioural state makes use of the "is" of definition.

When Place says that consciousness *is* a brain process, unlike the behaviourist, he is not making a claim about the *meaning* of mental assertions like "John feels pain." Instead, he is employing the "is" of composition; he is telling us what the sensation of pain is made of, or what that sensation really is. This claim should therefore be interpreted in the same way as assertions like "Lightning *is* a rapid electrical discharge" and "Heat *is* molecular kinetic energy." Both of these use the "is" of composition because they purport to tell us what lightning and heat really are. That is, science has shown convincingly that lightning is *nothing more than* an electrical discharge and that heat is *nothing more than* molecular kinetic energy. According to Place, the claim "Consciousness is a brain process" is no different. It claims that consciousness is *nothing more than* a brain process. To say that one sort of thing (e.g., heat, lightning, or pain) is really nothing more than another kind of thing (molecular kinetic energy, an electrical discharge, a brain process) is to *reduce* one kind of thing to another. Thus, these kinds of identity claims are said to be **reductive**.

According to Place, we should regard all three of these reductive identities as scientific hypotheses that should be justified in the same way as any other hypothesis. One form such justification can take is to discover correlations between the phenomena identified. For instance, if we discover through a series of tests that an electrical discharge is present every time we see lightning, then we have a reason for taking the hypothesis that lightning is an electrical discharge seriously. If lightning were rarely accompanied by an electrical discharge, there would be little reason to think the two are identical.

A second form of justification concerns the explanatory power of the proposed identity. If the anticipated reduction helps to explain certain facts about the phenomenon in question, then that is another reason to think the identity is genuine. For example, the hypothesis that lightning is a rapid electrical discharge explains why lightning appears as a bright flash of light, why it happens quickly, and why it causes thunder. Because the reduction of lightning to an electrical discharge explains all these facts about lightning, we have even more reason for thinking the identity is true. Place thinks we should employ these kinds of strategies to support the identification of sensations with brain processes. For instance, if the sensation of red is a brain state, then we ought to discover correlations between sensations of red and some kind of brain state. Furthermore, learning about that brain state and the physical processes that cause it should help to explain why the sensation of red feels like it does.

To some extent Place's prediction has come true. An interesting fact about our experience of colour is that we don't have reddish-green or yellowish-blue sensations. Of course we can see objects that are red with blue dots, and we can see someone mix together red and green pigment, but this is not the same thing as having a reddish-green sensation—having a continuous part of the visual field look uniformly red and green at the same time. Although there is never any part of your visual field that is simultaneously uniformly red-looking and green-looking or simultaneously uniformly yellow-looking and blue-looking, other combinations are possible. Continuous parts of your visual field can be simultaneously uniformly yellowish-red, greenish-blue, reddish-blue, and yellowish-green. What, if anything, explains these facts?

It turns out that there are two main neural pathways that send information about colour from the retina to the visual cortex. Red and green are transmitted by one pathway and yellow and blue by another. Each pathway sends information by being either excited or inhibited. If either pathway fires at its base rate (it is neither excited nor inhibited) the result is a sensation of grey. If the red-green pathway is excited while the yellow-blue pathway fires at its base rate, one has a reddish sensation. If it is inhibited while the other pathway fires at its base rate, one has a greenish sensation. The same thing holds for the yellow-blue pathway. If it is excited while the red-green pathway fires at its base rate, this produces a yellow sensation. If it is inhibited while the red-green pathway fires at its base rate, one has a blue sensation. Neither pathway can be simultaneously excited and inhibited. That is, the red-green pathway cannot transmit for both red and green at the same time. Similarly, the yellow-blue pathway cannot transmit for both yellow and blue at the same time. However, it is possible for both pathways to be excited or inhibited, or for one to be excited while the other is inhibited. These facts about the neural basis of colour experience seem to explain why our colour sensations have the kind of character they do. The neurology of colour vision explains why we can have greenish-yellow experiences but not reddish-green experiences. It also allows us to predict what kinds of experiences people would have if their pathways were artificially stimulated in certain ways. This, of course, is only one simple example of the kind of thing Place has in mind. While these kinds of facts coupled with mind-brain correlations do not *prove* that consciousness is a brain process, they do give us reasons for taking the hypothesis seriously, which is all Place can ask for.

As we saw, Place was careful to explain that when he said consciousness is a brain process, he was using the "is" of composition and so was not making an assertion about the *meaning* of our psychological vocabulary. Something else he should have emphasized but did not is the fact that his brand of identity theory asserts a relationship between mental and neural *types*. To understand this we need first to understand the difference between **types** and **tokens**. A type is a general kind of thing, like a group or a category. A token is a particular member of a type. For instance, *pain* is a type or kind of sensation that includes (among many others) the pain I felt on the morning I broke my arm when I was young and the pain you felt when the dentist removed your first wisdom tooth. Each of these is a *token* of the type *pain*. The reason type identity theorists formulate the identity between types is due to the fact that the evidence for the identity lies in correlations between mental states and brain states.

To illustrate this idea, let's use the example of a correlation between sensations of pain and a neural process such as C-fibre stimulation. Token pains occur only once because tokens are particular individuals. I cannot (thankfully) ever experience the same token pain I did when I broke my arm as a child. At best (or worst), I can break my arm again and feel another token pain that is similar to the one I felt when I was young, but that can't be the *same* pain any more than recreating Game Four of the 1993 World Series is playing the *same* baseball game. Correlations require repeated occurrences of phenomena. That is, in order to show that pain and C-fibre stimulation are correlated, we need to observe the two happening together over and over again. Because tokens only occur once, it is impossible to correlate them with anything. Instead, we need to correlate a collection of different pains with a collection of different instances of C-fibre stimulation. In this case, we are correlating two *types* or *kinds* of things: pain and C-fibre stimulation. On the basis of this kind of correlation, the identity theorist can only say that pain, as a kind of mental state, is identical with a kind of brain process—C-fibre stimulation. The reason this theory is called the **type identity theory** is because the proposed identity between the mental and the physical is an identity between types.

The Phenomenological Fallacy

When Place first presented the type identity theory, he anticipated the following kind of objection: sensations cannot be brain states because they have properties that do not exist in the brain or in the external world. Take, for instance, the sensation of an after-image. When one stares at a bright object such as a light bulb and then looks away, one has a green after-image in the visual field, although no bulb is present. The sensation itself has certain properties. It has a specific shape, a specific size, and a colour. Since, during the experience of an after-image there is no actual green object within view, it makes little sense to say that the properties of the after-image are properties of something in the external world. It also makes no sense to say that one's brain state has that shape, size, and colour, for brain states are not green or round. It seems, then, that the sensation—the bearer of these properties—must be something else altogether, something non-physical. At any rate, it certainly can't be a brain state, in which case the identity theory is false.

Place claims that this type of argument is guilty of an error which he calls the **phenomenological fallacy**. The error lies in assuming there is such a thing as a phenomenal field: an internal theatre of the mind with a stage occupied by sensations that are observed by the mind's eye. According to this assumption, the sensations on the stage must resemble the objects we claim to perceive in the world and thus must literally have shapes, colours, and sizes. According to Place, our reason for thinking there is a phenomenal field is that we have adopted a Cartesian picture of our relationship to the world around us. According to Descartes, what we know directly and with certainty are the contents of our minds, which, among other things, include sensations. The task for Descartes was to find a way to get from the knowledge of our sensations to knowledge of the objects in the world that cause them.

For Place, this gets things backwards. We are actually directly aware of the properties of objects in the world around us and learn to say that we have sensations of them. For instance, we directly observe grass that is green and then learn to say that we have a sensation of green when we look at grass. The greenness, then, is a property of the grass and not of the sensation.

How does this eliminate the problem of an after-image if there is no light bulb in the field of view to bear the properties we see? Place posits a simple physiological explanation. When one experiences a green after-image with a certain shape, one's brain is in the kind of state that it would ordinarily be in when one looks at a green object of that shape, size, and so on. The fact that one's brain is affected the way it normally is by green objects explains why one seems to see something green even though there is no green object in the vicinity. Once we recognize the phenomeno-logical fallacy for what it is, the so-called intrinsic properties of experience do not represent an obstacle to the claim that consciousness is a brain process, for we no longer require the idea that sensations themselves have such properties.

The Intensional Fallacy

J.J.C. Smart tried to defend Place's version of the identity theory from various objections that cropped up shortly after Place published it. Smart claims that most of these objections are guilty of an error in reasoning called the **intensional fallacy**. We already saw an example of this fallacy in our discussion of Cartesian dualism. It crops up in a similar way in discussions of the identity theory because Place's critics tried to use the law of the indiscernibility of identicals to argue that sensations cannot be brain states. According to this law, if and only if A and B have all the same properties in common, then they must be identical—they are really just one thing. Critics of Place's theory claimed that brain states and states of consciousness have different properties, and thus, according to the indis-cernibility of identicals, they must be distinct things. One argu-ment that Smart considered is the following. Since the average person can have intimate knowledge of his sensations without knowing anything at all about neurology, sensations cannot be identical to brain processes. We can make this argument more explicit by rewriting it as follows:

> The average person knows his own sensations intimately.
> The average person does not know his brain processes intimately.
> Therefore, sensations cannot be identical to brain processes.

We saw earlier that the intensional fallacy occurs when one treats a psychological attitude toward *A* as though it were a property of *A*. That is, if the property in the argument that supports the distinction between *A* and *B* consists in *A*'s or *B*'s being *known, thought of, perceived, recognized, or doubted,* then the argument commits the intensional fallacy. Because the properties identified in the premises of the above argument consist of being *known* as such, these are not real properties; they are relationships between the knower and the thing(s) known. Let's use a different example to make the problem with the argument a little clearer:

> Lois Lane does not love Clark Kent.
> Lois Lane loves Superman.
> Therefore, Clark Kent is not identical to Superman.

Since we all know that Clark Kent *is* Superman, we know there is something wrong with this argument. The problem is that whether or not Lois Lane loves Superman or Clark Kent is not a property of Clark Kent or of Superman and so cannot be used to distinguish the two. Loving or not loving is a mental property of Lois Lane herself, not a property of the man in question.

The same error of reasoning occurs in the argument against the identity theory. From the fact that the average person doesn't know anything about neurology, it doesn't follow that *what* she knows when she is aware of a sensation isn't a brain state. Like Lois Lane, we can have knowledge of all kinds of things while remaining ignorant of their true identities. Thus, when the average person knows she has a sensation of red, she does possess knowledge of a brain state; she doesn't realize it because she doesn't know that sensations of red are brain states.

Part of the reason Place's critics have raised objections like the one above is that they have failed to appreciate Place's distinction between the "is" of definition and the "is" of composition. If the claim "consciousness is a brain state" used the "is" of definition, then (for example) "sensation of pain" would have the same meaning as "C-fibre stimulation" in the way that "bachelor" has the same meaning as "unmarried male." This would certainly be strange, for an implication of such a claim would be that the person who knows nothing about neurology actually means "My C-fibres are firing" when he or she says "I have a sensation of pain," which is clearly absurd. Because Place's critics think the identity theory has this implication, it is no wonder they think the theory must be false. As we saw, however, Place did not claim to present a thesis about the *meaning* of phrases like "sensation of red." In his view, although "I have a sensation of pain" and "My C-fibres are firing" refer to the same thing, these sentences have different meanings, which is why the average person can truthfully say the former without meaning the latter. This is not unusual, for words that refer to the same thing *often* have different meanings. We have already seen an example. The words "Superman" and "Clark Kent" have different meanings but refer to the same individual, which explains why Lois Lane saying "I love Superman" would mean something different from her saying "I love Clark Kent." We do not need to explore the reason for this here. For our purposes it is enough to appreciate that this sort of thing is possible. Once we acknowledge this and appreciate that Place's version of the identity theory is not a claim about the meaning of our mental vocabulary, it becomes clear that the objection is misplaced.

Reductionism and the Unity of Science

Ten or 15 years after Place first proposed the identity theory, other philosophers took his idea and reformulated it in the light of recent developments in the philosophy of science. In the 1950s and 1960s many philosophers adopted a model of science according to which the different branches of scientific inquiry, such as biology, chemistry, and physics, could be unified into a grand scientific system. They referred to this as the **unity of science.** These philosophers thought of the world as being layered or as having different levels. If we pick one level and then zoom in on it in greater detail to examine its parts, we arrive at the next, more detailed level. The basic levels of the world were (in descending order of detail) thought to be as follows: social groups, living things, cells, molecules, atoms, elementary particles. The unity of science involved the idea that because each level can be broken down into parts and that these parts constitute the level below it (i.e., social groups are made up of individual living things, which are made up of cells, etc.), there is a hierarchy of disciplines that correspond to these basic levels in the world, each of which studies the same phenomena at a more detailed level of specificity than the one above it. What was required was a way to connect the scientific disciplines that correspond to each of these levels.

The main proposal for how to achieve unity in the sciences was that each branch of science could be connected to the one below it by means of an **intertheoretic reduction**. That is, it was suggested that a theory like biology could be *reduced* to the next more basic theory, chemistry; that chemistry could be reduced to atomic theory; and so on. The reduction of one theory to another would involve showing that the terms and laws of both theories talk about the same phenomena but at different levels of detail and with different vocabularies. Crucial to this reduction is the formulation of **bridge laws** that connect the two theories together. For example, if scientists discovered that whenever a cell has a certain feature x, it also has chemical feature y, and does so without exception, this is evidence of a law connecting these two characteristics. This law would take the form "x if and only if y" and would serve as a bridge between biology and chemistry. Once a sufficient number of these bridge laws are discovered, scientists could then show that the laws and relations that make up cellular biology are mirrored in the more fundamental laws and relations that make up chemistry. This would pave the way for a smooth reduction of cellular biology to chemistry. Once one theory is reduced to another, it would become possible to make accurate deductions about higher level phenomena from facts described at lower levels. For instance, if cellular biology were reduced to chemistry, scientists would be able to predict what would happen at the cellular level from knowledge of the chemical facts plus the relevant bridge laws.

Identity theorists began to reformulate the identity theory in terms of this concept of intertheoretic reduction that was so central to the unity of science. While Place insisted that the identity theory amounted to the claim that mental states are composed of brain states, these new theorists proposed that the identity theory is really a claim about the possibility of reducing one *theory* to another—in this case, of reducing psychology to neurology. Psychology and neurology are both theories, each with their own vocabulary and their own laws and principles. Just as the reduction of cellular biology to chemistry involves discovering laws connecting these two theories, to reduce psychology to neurology it would be necessary to discover laws connecting psychology and neurology. Because these laws hold between the psychological states described by psychology and the physical states described by neurology, these were called **psychophysical laws**. Once enough of these psychophysical bridge laws are in place to see how the laws of psychology are mirrored in the laws of neurology, we have successfully reduced the former theory to the latter. Just as the reduction of cellular biology to chemistry shows that cells are really nothing more than chemical compounds, the reduction of psychology to neurology would show that mental states are nothing more than neurological states and, hence, are physical phenomena that can be understood and explained by the physical sciences. The successful reduction of psychology to neurology would, at least in principle, allow scientists to deduce facts about psychology from a possession of the neurological facts plus the relevant psychophysical bridge laws.

Problems for Type Identity Theory

Despite its initial popularity, philosophers have identified several serious philosophical problems with the type identity theory. We will focus on two of these in this section. The first line of criticism focuses on the unity of science which was so influential in shaping later versions of the type identity theory. Philosophers like Ian Hacking have argued that the idea of scientific theories being united by sets of bridge laws into a continuous hierarchical system was overly optimistic and has not been borne out by scientific practice. As the various branches of natural science have developed, we have not seen a trend toward the unification of scientific theories. In fact, we have seen just the opposite. Different branches of science are increasingly specialized and more isolated from one another than ever before. We have not seen intertheoretic reductions of higher level theories to more basic physical theories and hence have seen little evidence of a trend toward the unification of science. Since the identity theory depends in part on the concept of intertheoretic reduction—an important stage in the unification of the sciences—the existing lack of unity in the sciences makes the reduction of psychology to neurology seem very implausible.

Advocates of the identity theory would likely respond to this complaint by suggesting that there is only so much one can conclude from the actual practice of science. The fact that scientific practice seems to be moving away from a unified theory need not have any genuine implications for the type identity theory. It could be that the recent trend toward fragmentation is the result of social factors (perhaps connected to the way research is funded) as opposed to purely scientific progress and, thus, that scientific practice might yet change and develop in the way philosophers predicted. Given these kinds of considerations, defenders of the type identity theory claim it is premature to draw conclusions about the plausibility of the theory based on observations about the current state of scientific practice.

While the first criticism affects only the later versions of the identity theory, the second line of criticism applies equally well to both early and later versions. To appreciate this criticism we need to remember what the identity theorist is saying when she claims that a mental state like pain can be reduced to a physical state like the firing of C-fibres. To say this is not to say that pain and C-fibre stimulation are correlated, but that pain *just is* C-fibre stimulation. This has the implication that the occurrence of pain is impossible without C-fibre stimulation, for they are the very same thing described in different ways. To see this, try to imagine Ralph Lauren and Ralph Lifshitz being identical but being in two different places at the same time. Such a thing is clearly impossible. Because the type identity theorist thinks all types of mental states are really types of physical states, the same reasoning holds for these as well. For instance, if the sensation of pain is a type of brain state, then it would be impossible for something without that brain state to have sensations of pain. This implication creates serious problems for the type identity theory when combined with the phenomenon of neural plasticity and with an idea called the principle of multiple realization.

Neural plasticity is an interesting feature of the brain. Studies have shown that when one part of the human brain is destroyed, other parts can sometimes take over the functions of the destroyed parts. This ability is much more pronounced in younger brains than in older ones, which is why a stroke victim at the age of 60 is less likely to recover lost motor functions and cognitive capacities than someone who has a stroke at age 20. This also explains the remarkable ability of children who are born with large portions of their brains missing to grow into perfectly normal adults. When we combine the phenomenon of neural plasticity with the observation about reduction, it spells trouble for the type identity theorist. The difficulty is that if one part of the brain can assume the functions of another part, there is reason to be sceptical of reductive claims about the mental states associated with those functions. Let's use a rather extreme and fictitious example to illustrate the point.

The identity theorist wants to say, for example, that the auditory sensation of ringing bells is identical to a brain state in the primary sensory cortex, which we will call brain state x. Now imagine an individual whose brain is incapable of being stimulated in that way because, due to some kind of severe neural damage, the necessary part of the brain is missing. According to neural plasticity, it is possible for this person to have the sensation of hearing ringing bells if another part of the brain compensates for the damaged area. If this is possible, then the identity theorist is in serious trouble. Hearing the sound of ringing bells cannot be identical to brain state x if there is an individual who hears that sound but does so by being in a completely different brain state. Since it is possible to have this sensation without being in brain state x, the sensation of hearing ringing bells cannot be identical with that brain state. It is conceivable that this could happen with any kind of mental state whatsoever, in which case the reductive theory of mind looks very implausible.

The second problem for the type identity theory is closely related to the one we just discussed, but takes things somewhat farther. Critics have suggested that the identity theory is guilty of a kind of chauvinism. By identifying mental states with the brain states of human beings, the theory precludes the possibility of other forms of life having mental states like ours. The nature of this complaint can be fairly mild or quite exotic. For instance, octopi and other earthly creatures have brains that are very different from ours, yet we might want to say that they can feel pain just like we do. Since, according to the type identity theory, pain is a kind of brain state and since octopi have brains that are quite unlike ours, an implication of the type identity theory is that it must be impossible for octopi to feel pain, which seems implausible to many.

More fanciful formulations of this complaint say that there could be intelligent creatures on other planets (Martians) who are capable of all the same mental states as us but who are completely different from us physically. For instance, they might be silicon-based life forms instead of carbon-based. If Martians feel pain but don't even have brains, then the type identity theory must be false. These cases raise problems for the identity theory in a similar way as the phenomenon of neural plasticity. In either case, we have beings that are capable of being in the same mental states but are incapable of being in the same brain states. If mental states are just brain states, as the identity theorist claims, this should not be possible.

These kinds of considerations have motivated philosophers (e.g., Jerry Fodor) to adopt an idea called **the principle of**

multiple realization. According to this principle, mental states are *multiply realizable*. This means that the same type or kind of mental state, such as the sensation of pain, can exist in a variety of different complex physical systems. Thus, it is possible for human beings, octopi, Martians, and other forms of life to share the same kinds of mental states even though they might have *nothing* in common at the physical level. This principle is in obvious tension with the type identity theory for the reasons described above and has led many philosophers to abandon the identity theory as a viable theory of mind. If there is no one physical state common to all beings that feel pain, pain cannot be reduced to a physical state in the way the identity theorists proposed.

Some identity theorists (e.g., Jaegwon Kim) have responded to this objection by arguing that the principle of multiple realization is not actually at odds with a reductive theory of mind. Typically, they claim that if we examine other successful cases of reduction, we will appreciate the fact that the identity theory is perfectly consistent with multiple realization. One of the most successful and influential cases of reduction was that of temperature to molecular kinetic energy. It turns out, however, that the reductive claim *heat is molecular kinetic energy* is an oversimplification that is strictly true only for gases. Like pain, temperature is something that is also multiply realizable. Vacuums and plasmas, for instance, do not contain constituent molecules, yet they are said to have temperatures. Depending on whether we are talking about a solid, a gas, a vacuum, or a plasma, temperature turns out to be a different kind of thing.

The conclusion we should draw from this observation is that ontological reductions are specific to a given domain—they are relative. If our best examples of successful reductions are relative, then we should not expect the reduction of mind to matter to be any different. This means the identity theorist is correct when she says pain is a physical state, but we should expect pain to be identical to a different physical state depending on whether we are talking about humans, Martians, or octopi. In humans pain will be one kind of brain state, in Martians pain will be some kind of silicon state, and in octopi pain will be yet another kind of physical state. This means we cannot assert reductive identities broadly (e.g., *pain is identical to brain state x*). Instead, we should express reductive identities more narrowly (e.g., *pain in a human is brain state x*).

This might be an effective way to deal with multiple realization when one's concern is with mental kinds that are common to different species, but it does not appear to address the first problem we explored above. We observed that there are non-standard physical realizations of mental kinds in human beings because of neural plasticity; thus, there is reason to believe it is possible for human beings to share the same kinds of mental states without sharing the same kinds of brain states. This means that even the species-relative identity claims suggested above are problematic. If pain can be realized differently among individual humans, we can't even say *pain in a human is identical to brain state x*. Similarly, if we assume neural plasticity (or its equivalent) is possible in Martians and other creatures, we cannot say with confidence that *pain in a Martian is identical to silicon state x*.

The obvious solution to this problem is to narrow the domain of the reductions even further and to relativize them to individuals instead of species. In this case identity theorists would have to say that *pain in Paul is brain state x* and *pain in Mary is brain state y*. Similarly, when it comes to other species, they would have to say that *pain in Mike the Martian is silicon state x*, whereas *pain in Matilda the Martian is silicon state y*. However, even this might not work. Suppose Paul suffers a serious head injury and loses the ability to be in brain state *x*. Fortunately Paul is fairly young, so his brain adapts to the damage, and some other set of neurons takes over for the injured area. Paul once again has the ability to feel pain, but does so without being in brain state *x*; instead, he is in brain state *y*. In light of this possibility, the identity theorist needs not only to relativize identity claims to individuals, but also to *times*. Thus, a more appropriate formulation of the identity claim would be to say *pain in Paul at time t is brain state x*.

Once the identity claims become this specific, it is unclear whether or not we have a reductive theory of mind any more. As we saw, the point of an ontological reduction was to show that one kind of thing (a mental kind) is really just another kind of thing (a physical kind); for instance, that pain is really just C-fibre stimulation. When identities are relativized down to particular individuals at particular times, identity theorists seem to lose the spirit of the intended identity. Under these conditions, they do not appear to be telling us what pain really is, for pain seems to be something different depending on what kind of thing we are talking about and when we are talking about it. At any rate, the identity theorists are no longer saying what pain, as a kind or type of thing is, but what individual token pains really are. To do this is arguably to abandon type identity in favour of a token identity theory.

There are a number of philosophers who think these criticisms are not very compelling or can be answered in one of the ways identified. Thus, the identity theory still has its followers. By and large, however, philosophers tend to think the principle of multiple realization is a genuine obstacle to conceiving of the identity between the mental and the physical as an identity between types. Thus, most materialists have searched for an alternative way to express the identity between the mental and the physical. Two of the most influential of these are found in the next two theories we will discuss: functionalism and anomalous monism.

Suggestions for Further Reading

Churchland, P. 1979. *Scientific Realism and the Plasticity of Mind*. Cambridge: Cambridge University Press.

Nagel, E. 1961. *The Structure of Science*. New York: Harcourt, Brace, and World.

Place, U.T. 1956. "Is Consciousness a Brain Process?" *British Journal of Psychology* 47: 44–50.

Putnam, H., and P. Oppenheim. 1958. "The Unity of Science as a Working Hypothesis." *Minnesota Studies in the Philosophy of Science: Volume II*. Ed. H. Feigl, M. Scriven, and G. Maxwell. Minneapolis, MN: University of Minnesota Press.

Smart, J.J.C. 1959. "Sensations and Brain Processes." *Philosophical Review* 68: 141–56.

CHAPTER 4

FUNCTIONALISM

Functional Definitions

When we try to understand things in the world we often find it more helpful to talk about the function or purpose they serve than to examine their physical properties or characteristics. Imagine that someone asked you to define a chair. What would you say? A good definition should be neither too broad nor too narrow; that is, a definition ought not to include things that should be excluded or exclude things that should be included. For example, if I were to define squirrels as furry animals that live in trees, this definition would be both too broad and too narrow. It is too broad because other furry animals aside from squirrels such as racoons live in trees, and we don't want to have to say that racoons are actually squirrels. The definition is also too narrow because it excludes squirrels that live in attics in urban areas. If we were to accept the definition as stated, we would have to conclude that such animals are not really squirrels by virtue of where they live, which is clearly absurd. When formulating a definition of the word "chair" then, you must ensure that the definition does not include things that aren't really chairs and that it doesn't exclude things most of us would consider to be chairs.

Chairs vary widely both in their design and in the materials out of which they are constructed. They can be made of wood, a single piece of moulded plastic, metal, wicker, or a number of other substances. They can also look very different. A leather wing-backed chair has a very different design and tends to be much more comfortable than the chair you sit in at your average university lecture. While most chairs have four legs, not all of them do; some have five metal or plastic castors instead, others are designed like tripods, and there are additional possibilities. In light of these facts, to define what a chair is you would probably not want to say anything about what chairs are made of or what they look like, for the minute you begin to characterize a chair as something made of wood or something with four legs you exclude all the chairs in the world made out of different materials with different designs, rendering your definition excessively narrow. Therefore, you are better off defining a chair in terms of its function: as something designed for people to sit on. This functional definition captures something that is true of all chairs regardless of what they are made of or how they look.

Functional definitions are very common. We use them to understand all kinds of things, from bodily organs (e.g., the heart is an organ that pumps blood through the body) to the parts of a car (e.g., brakes are a mechanism that allows a vehicle to decelerate and stop). When we define something in terms of its function we typically focus our attention on its use or purpose. To identify the function or purpose of something involves an implicit reference to certain causal relationships. That is, when we define something like a chair in terms of its function, part of our understanding involves the idea that chairs play a certain kind of **causal role**. When human beings place their weight on them (a cause), chairs support their bodies in a seated position so that human beings don't fall down (an effect). This causal role is common to all chairs (at least, all successful ones) regardless of what they look like or what they are made of, which is why it is more helpful to define what a chair is in terms of what it does than in terms of its design or composition. This is not to say that functional definitions like this are without their problems. They often can appear to be too broad. The seat in a car or in a boat would satisfy the functional definition of a chair, yet it is unclear whether or not we would want to call such things chairs. Of course, any definition (functional or otherwise) will encounter these kinds of borderline cases. It is more important for a definition not to be excessively narrow, and functional definitions satisfy this criterion better than most.

The Functional Theory of Mind

In the previous chapter we saw that one of the obstacles to the type identity theory was the idea that mental states are multiply realizable. That is, there is reason to suspect that the very same kinds of mental states of which we are capable (e.g., pains) can occur in creatures that are radically different from us at the physical level. In light of the principle of multiple realization, functionalists conceded that it would be impossible to identify pain with any one kind of physical state, for it is extremely unlikely that a silicon-based life form could have any physical states in common with a human being. This is similar to the problem with trying to define what a chair is by referring to its physical properties. Just as there is no one set of physical traits or properties common to all chairs, there is no one set of physical traits or properties common to all pains. Since the functional definition of a chair identifies something common to all chairs in spite of their physical diversity, functionalists proposed that a functional characterization of mental states could succeed where the identity theory failed. Perhaps a functional account of pain could identify something common to all pains, regardless of whether we are talking about pain in a human, in a Martian, or in some other kind of creature.

As we have seen, functional definitions characterize phenomena in terms of their causal roles. Thus, to adopt a functional account of a mental state like pain requires understanding the causal role of pain. In large part this involves a description of the typical causes and effects of pain. We know, for instance, that pain tends to be caused by bodily injury and that it in turn causes various forms of pain-behaviour, such as yelling, withdrawing the injured part of the body from the stimulus, and so on. The functional account of pain, then, defines it as a state with these kinds of causes and effects. Thus, to be in pain is to be in a state that is caused by bodily injury and that causes pain-behaviour. This is a far more abstract account of pain than the one offered by the identity theory because no mention is made of the way in which pain is realized. The identity theory attempts to define pain in terms of its **intrinsic properties**—the physical characteristics pain has in itself as a neural or silicon event. To define pain in terms of its causes and effects is to define it in terms of its **extrinsic properties**—its relations to other things such as stimuli and behaviour. Thus, it is often said that functionalism defines mental states as **abstract organizational states** of complex systems. Again, the reason for this is the principle of multiple realization: if we tried to define pain by identifying its intrinsic physical properties, our definition would be true only of a particular species or possibly only of a particular member of that species at a particular time, in which case our definition would be too narrow. By defining pain in terms of its extrinsic properties, we avoid this problem because the same causes and effects can occur in radically different physical systems, be they human beings or Martians. Even if Martians have bodies made of silicon, they can, like us, still suffer bodily damage and engage in pain-behaviour.

Functionalism is often described as the heir to behaviourism because the functional account of mental states is similar to the behaviourist account. Both theories treat mental states like pain as a complex set of behaviour that occurs under certain conditions, and neither theory has much to say about the physical underpinnings of that behaviour. Functionalism differs from behaviourism in two crucial respects, however. The first and most obvious difference is that the behaviourists vehemently denied that pain is an *inner cause* of behaviour and identified it with behaviour itself (or the disposition to behave in that way). While functionalists share with the behaviourists the idea that behaviour is important for understanding mental states like pain, the functionalists think pain is only *partially* defined in terms of behaviour. In addition, functionalists *also* think of pain as an inner state that causes pain-behaviour.

The second way in which functionalism differs from behaviourism concerns the role of other mental states in the functional account of the mind. Functionalists claim that the extrinsic relations that define a mental state like pain include not only the causes and behavioural effects of pain, but also include *other mental states*. To appreciate the significance of this we need to remember that, according to behaviourism, we should be able to abandon our psychological vocabulary and replace it, without loss of meaning, with a behavioural vocabulary since when we talk about mental states what we are really referring to is behaviour. As we saw in Chapter 2, there is good reason to expect such a project to fail because any analysis of mental states in terms of behavioural dispositions retains some residue of mentality. The functionalists were keenly aware of this problem. They realized that any account of mental states in terms of stimuli and behaviour (or *input* and *output*) could succeed only if other mental states were mentioned as well. Thus, functionalists defined pain as a functional state the typical cause of which is bodily damage and the typical effects of which include pain-behaviour *plus* a variety of other mental states, such as aversion, fear, anger, anxiety, and so on. The advantage of incorporating other mental states into the functional analysis of the mind is that doing so avoids the problem that was so devastating to behaviourism.

So far we have only seen an example of how functionalists account for sensations like pain. What do they say about propositional attitudes? For functionalists, beliefs, desires, and other propositional attitudes are also functional states, and thus should be understood in terms of their causal roles. For example, my friend Marvin, an alien from another planet who is made of silicon, and I can both believe that it is about to rain. By hypothesis, we share no intrinsic physical properties since Marvin doesn't even have a brain. However, there are extrinsic properties we have in common. Our sensory systems are both affected by light waves reflecting off the clouds in the sky. We both utter "It's going to rain," and we both reach for our umbrellas. In addition to these commonalities, we also share other mental states under these circumstances. For example, we both believe that if it rains and we don't have our umbrellas, we will get wet. We also both have a desire not to get wet. According to the functionalist, our belief that it is going to rain is this abstract organizational state with the identified causal role: the state that is caused by the light waves reflected by the clouds and that causes the mentioned behaviour and associated beliefs and desires.

Functionalism is usually portrayed as a form of physicalism, though strictly speaking it is ontologically neutral, meaning that it allows for the possibility of either physicalism or dualism. The reason it is ontologically neutral is that functionalism says nothing about how functional states are realized because of its commitment to multiple realization. Since mental states are multiply realizable, they can be realized in physically diverse bodies or possibly even in non-physical souls. Despite this, however, functionalists are *usually* physicalists because they believe that, when it comes to human beings, functional states are physically realized by our bodies and central nervous systems. Furthermore, as we saw in Chapter 2 in our discussion of the problem of interaction, there is good reason to be sceptical of the idea that a non-physical substance could realize the required causal roles since these roles include causal connections to physical behaviour. A non-physical soul, then, is ill-equipped to serve as the realizer for mental states. Thus, so long as a functionalist claims that the functional states with which mental states are identical are physically realized, functionalism is a form of physicalism.

Functionalism and Artificial Intelligence

The functionalist claim that mental states can be realized in physically different ways created a new interest among philosophers in the possibility of **artificial intelligence** (AI). If the functionalists are correct and a complex system does not require an organic brain like ours in order to have mental states, then perhaps a sufficiently complicated computer could have a mind. Furthermore, functional states are quite similar to the computational states of computers running programs. In both cases there is some kind of input, there is an internal processing of the information, and there is the resulting output. So long as a computer and its program are capable of realizing the causal roles corresponding to the relationships between stimuli, other mental states, and resulting behaviour in human beings, the computer would have all the same functional states we do. For instance, if you could program a computer with a robot body to look at the sky, say "It's going to rain," reach for its umbrella, and form other related beliefs, then the computer really would believe it is going to rain.

John Searle distinguishes between two conceptions of artificial intelligence, which he calls **strong** and **weak AI**. Strong AI is the thesis described above. According to this view, if a computer can successfully imitate human intelligence by realizing states that play the same causal role as our own mental states, then the computer actually *is* a mind. By contrast, weak AI is the claim that computer modeling of the human mind might give us some genuine insight into the way the human mind works but that such models are not themselves conscious intelligent minds.

Suppose someone claimed to have succeeded at creating artificial intelligence. How could we determine that their computer actually is a conscious mind? Most supporters of strong AI claim that we should use something called the **Turing Test**, named after Alan Turing, a mathematician and code breaker who was one of the first to take the idea of AI seriously. According to the Turing Test, if a computer successfully mimics human intelligence, then it actually *is* intelligent. The test involves the following. A willing subject is given a computer console and told they can use it to communicate with something in an adjacent room: either another person or a computer. They can ask their interlocutor any questions they want by using a keyboard and they can read responses on a computer screen. If by the end of the conversation the subject cannot tell that they have been interacting with a computer program instead of with another person, then the computer actually has a mind. If the participant can tell that there isn't really anybody at the other end responding to the questions, then the computer fails the Turing Test and is not intelligent and so has no mind.

The reason the Turing Test seemed like a good way to tell if a computer has a mind is that it employs the same criteria we ordinarily use when interacting with other persons. The only evidence we have at our disposal to show that other people have minds, as we saw in Chapter 2, is their behaviour. Thus, when we determine whether or not something non-human has a mind our criteria should not be significantly different. Of course, some differences are required. Since computers do not have bodies like ours (not yet, anyway), our criteria cannot depend on such things as specific bodily movements. If this seems to grant the advocate of strong AI too much, consider what the functionalist is committed to by accepting multiple realization. An intelligent form of life on some distant planet might not have any of the physical features that would permit the kind of bodily behaviour we take as evidence of intelligence among human beings. For instance, such creatures might be jelly-like formless blobs that cannot point, make facial expressions, nod, and so on. However, if they could communicate with us by interfacing with a computer and generating script in English, we would have no doubt that they are intelligent. In the Turing Test we are limited to one form of behaviour only: written responses to questions. While this is a more restricted set of criteria than the ones we would ordinarily use, in light of our intelligent blob from another planet we can appreciate how appropriate very limited behavioural criteria might be.

The Chinese Room Argument

John Searle offered a now famous argument against the claims of strong AI. The goal of the argument is to undermine the Turing Test by showing that it is possible for a complex system to mimic intelligence without possessing any genuine understanding. If this is the case, then there is good reason to be sceptical of strong AI's claim that simulated intelligence *is* intelligence.

Searle asks you to imagine that you are locked in a room and that you don't know how to read Chinese characters. Periodically, a card is dropped into the room via a slot in the wall. On it is a question written in Chinese. You have no idea what the characters on the card mean, but you have at your disposal an elaborate system of files that together constitute the grammatical rules of the Chinese language. You also have at your disposal a set of easy-to-follow instructions, which tell you that, if you receive a card with a certain string of symbols on it, you should look in a specific folder and then copy the string of symbols displayed there on to a card and to push the card out through the slot in the wall. The symbols you copy on to the card are the correct answers to the questions you received as input. At no point in this procedure are the Chinese characters translated into English. All that has happened is that by following a set of instructions based on syntactic rules (the grammar of Chinese) you have provided grammatically correct responses to questions. Searle says that from the point of view of an external observer who asks the questions and reads the responses, whoever is inside the room will appear to understand Chinese. However, from your point of view, there is no understanding of Chinese at all. Any such understanding is an illusion. You haven't a clue what the questions or answers mean. All you did was follow a lot of rules about which symbols go with which.

Your interaction with the input, the system of rules, and the output is no different from a computer running a program and is intended to be a **counterexample** to strong AI. A counterexample is an instance that proves a view or claim is false. In this case we have a system that passes the Turing Test and thus that mimics an understanding of Chinese, but doesn't really understand Chinese. This shows that the Turing Test is not a reliable method of determining whether or not something is intelligent, in which case the claims of strong AI appear overly optimistic. Searle's conclusion is that a computer program is a mere **syntactic engine**. It can follow all the rules of a language and thus formulate appropriate answers to any question one might think of, but the computer never *understands* anything. To understand Chinese is to know what the symbols mean, not merely to be able to put strings of symbols together according to the rules of that language. What symbols mean is often called **semantics** and is contrasted with **syntax** or the grammatical rules of a language. Searle's view is that computer programs can be very good at syntax but have no grasp of semantics; they can manipulate symbols according to the rules of a language, but they can never understand what those symbols mean. Understanding must be something over and above the symbol manipulation of a computer program. In Searle's view, it is likely the result of certain special causal powers of the brain.

Advocates of strong AI have responded to Searle in numerous ways. A common answer is to say that while it is true that the person in the room does not understand Chinese, the system as a whole does. Searle has focused his attention only on one part of a complex system and has assumed that since this one part (the person in the room) does not understand Chinese, the entire system lacks this understanding too. This inference clearly does not follow. To see why, consider the following. I understand that there is a computer screen in front of me now. My understanding depends on a vast number of things, including the fact that my retinas are being stimulated in a certain way. I think it is very implausible to suggest that my retinas *understand* that there is a computer screen in front of me, but it doesn't follow from this that *I* lack this understanding. I am a very complex system and process information at many different levels in different ways. Just because one component involved in this information processing lacks understanding doesn't mean that the whole system does too. Thus, from the fact that the person in the Chinese room doesn't understand Chinese it does not follow that the entire complex system, of which the person in the room is only one part, doesn't understand Chinese.

Problems for Functionalism

Like its behaviourist predecessors, functionalism is often attacked on the grounds that it fails to provide an adequate account of the qualitative character of our sensations. There are two main forms of this objection. The first is called the **inverted spectrum argument**. The second is a variation on

John Searle's Chinese room argument and is called the **absent qualia argument**. The aim of both arguments (advanced by Ned Block) is to drive a wedge between functional organization and qualitative character in a way that proves qualia cannot be functional states. Both arguments try to achieve this by showing that it is possible for two functionally identical individuals to have different qualia. Since qualia are mental states, which are supposed to be functional states, different qualia ought to require different functional states. Thus, if two individuals can be functionally identical and yet have different mental states, mental states must be something more than functional states.

The first form this objection takes is the inverted spectrum argument. Have you ever wondered if the world looks different to other people in a way that is not discoverable? Perhaps you have imagined that the colours other people see are qualitatively different from the ones you see. The inverted spectrum argument makes use of this idea to undermine functionalism. It asks us to imagine the following possibility. Suppose that Jane and Anna are functionally identical interior designers with respect to their interaction with coloured objects. This means that when they are each presented with coloured objects, they both respond in the same way. For instance, when in the presence of something red, they make utterances such as "That's red"; they can both reliably differentiate between red objects and green objects; they agree that green tends to be a more soothing colour than red, that red is more like orange than blue, that deep red paint in the living room would go a lot better with the purple furniture than orange paint would, and so on. Jane and Anna, then, never disagree in their claims, judgements, or feelings about colour. Now in addition to this, imagine that Jane's colour experiences are inverted relative to Anna's. That is, when presented with a coloured object, Jane has the kind of experience Anna has when she looks at something that is its opponent colour. For example, when Jane looks at a red object, she has the kind of experience Anna has when she looks at green objects. If Jane looks at a blue object, she has a sensation like the one Anna has when she looks at an orange, and so on.

If the inversion of Jane's colour qualia is systematic, there should be no way for anyone to discover the differences between her sensations and Anna's. All of the relationships between the colours such as similarity, opposition, harmony, dissonance, contrast, and so on, are preserved, which is why Jane and Anna agree about which colours go with which when they decorate people's homes. Another factor that makes this state of affairs seem possible is the fact that we learn colour words by **ostension**—by *being shown* coloured objects. For instance, Jane and Anna both learned what the word "red" means by being shown red objects when they were children. Since red objects appear to Jane as green objects do to Anna, she has associated the word "red" with her sensations of green and thus says that red objects are red even though they appear to her the way green objects appear to everyone else.

If we admit that such a state of affairs represents a coherent possibility, this creates a serious problem for functionalism. The sensation of red is a mental state and, according to functionalists, must be a functional state that occupies a certain causal role. The functionalist, then, is committed to the idea that Jane's colour qualia do not matter. So long as she responds in the

appropriate way to red objects and has the right sort of associated mental states, she is having a sensation of red even if it is
accompanied by a green quale. Many people find this idea difficult to accept. It seems obvious to them that if someone has a
sensation with a green quale—a sensation that has a felt greenish quality—then even if that sensation is caused by something
red and produces utterances such as "That's red," the sensation
itself is *really* a sensation of green. The qualitative character of
a sensation seems to take priority over its functional relationships. Philosophers who agree with this idea must conclude that
functionalism is false, for the functionalist must maintain the
opposite: that what makes a sensation the sensation it is isn't
the quale associated with it, but are the functional or causal
relationships in which the sensation is embedded.

One way for the functionalist to reply to this objection is to
offer reasons for thinking that the functional role of a sensation should take priority over its quale. The most convincing
route to this conclusion involves reflection on our means of
grouping sensations together as sensations of the same kind.
Those who accept the inverted spectrum argument assume
that we group sensations together as sensations of the same
kind or type in virtue of a common phenomenal property or
quale. Functionalists claim this assumption is false. Consider
for a moment all the sensations we classify as pain. Now think
about the difference in the way some of these pains feel from
one another. For instance, consider how different the burn
from grabbing the handle of a hot pan feels from the sensation
of a tooth ache. Compare the sensation of a bad migraine with
that of a whistle blown loudly next to one's ear. All these experiences have quite diverse qualitative characters, and yet we

speak of them all uniformly as pains. Given the differences in the phenomenal feel of these sensations, it seems implausible to insist that they nevertheless have a common quale in virtue of which we group them together as pains. Yet this is precisely what the advocate of spectrum inversion asks us to accept by claiming that the nature of a sensation depends entirely on its intrinsic character. If we reject this view, then we must concede that the reason we group these sensations together as pains is because of their common *functional* features. They all involve actual or potential bodily damage; they produce an involuntary withdrawal from the stimulus along with certain kinds of vocal behaviour; and they cause mental states such as anxiety, dislike, and distraction.

The functionalist will claim that in light of these considerations the inverted spectrum argument loses its force as an objection to functionalism. If our reflections on the way we group together sensations of pain are correct, then we should expect the same to be true of other sensations, including sensations of colour. Thus, someone has a sensation of red as long as they are in the appropriate functional state, regardless of the intrinsic character of the sensation. The functionalist, then, has given us reasons for thinking that Jane really does have a sensation of red when she looks at red objects even though her sensation has the qualitative character of Anna's sensation when she looks at something green. This might still strike you as implausible because there remains an important mental difference between Jane and Anna that is not captured by a functional characterization of their mental states. Functionalists, however, are comfortable with this and claim such differences are more common than we might suspect. Given the fact that no two human brains develop in precisely the same way, there is reason to think that functional states are physically realized in slightly different ways in different individuals, and it is likely that these physical differences have an impact on the qualitative character of their sensations. Thus, because the sensation of red is realized in Jane in a slightly different way than it is realized in Anna, Jane's sensations of red might feel different from Anna's. When we introduce the idea of creatures from other planets who realize the sensation of red in *radically* different ways, we should expect their sensations of red to feel very different from ours. Thus, functionalists could claim we should embrace the idea described by the inverted spectrum argument and should consequently recognize that it poses no threat to functionalism at all.

This reply to the problem of inverted qualia depends on our willingness to let qualia fall out of the picture of what matters when we talk about our mental states. While this approach might work for some, one should wonder whether or not this downgrading of the importance of qualia really addresses the problem for the functionalist. Even if it is true that we individuate our mental states according to functional criteria, one might argue that the inverted spectrum argument nevertheless identifies a mental difference in the absence of a functional difference. To the opponent of functionalism, this is the crucial point, whatever role qualia might play in the individuation of our mental states. As long as there can be a mental difference without a functional difference, mental states cannot be identical to functional states.

The appeal to multiple realization and the claims about the way in which we categorize our sensations may or may not address the possibility of functionally equivalent systems with different qualia. However, you might think that if something lacks qualia *entirely* it would be a mistake to say that it has sensations at all. This is the idea behind the second objection to functionalism—the *absent qualia argument*. In it, we are asked to imagine a being that is functionally identical to a normal human except that it lacks qualia entirely. Philosophers often refer to such beings as **zombies**. These are not the zombies you may have seen in Hollywood movies that run amok trying to eat the brains of their victims. The philosopher's zombie acts *exactly* like a normal, conscious person but is completely unconscious and thus has no qualia. Although zombies are unconscious, they are nevertheless informationally sensitive, meaning that they can detect objects in the world via their senses, but do so in a way that lacks qualitative character. To understand what this means, consider the behaviour of a thermostat. It has the ability to detect when the temperature of the room is too low and thus is sensitive to certain kinds of information about its environment. However, when a thermostat detects this information, there is nothing that it is like for the thermostat to do this; there are no qualia accompanying this informational sensitivity. We do not ordinarily think that thermostats are conscious. Thus, the thermostat detects information in the environment but does so in a way that does not involve any qualia. Zombies are like very complicated thermostats. They are sensitive to a vast array of information about the world around them, but it is not like anything for zombies to be sensitive to this information. They have no qualia at all.

Let us suppose, then, that I have a zombie twin who is functionally just like me. If you prick us both on the finger with a pin, we enter the same kind of functional states. We both respond with the same behaviour: we say "Ouch," quickly withdraw our fingers from the pin, and stick our fingers in our mouths. If you ask me and my twin "Do you like being pricked with pins?" we would respond by saying "No." Since my twin and I are in a state with the same causal or functional role, we must be in the same kind of mental state: we must both be having a sensation of pain.

In comparison to the inverted spectrum argument, it is harder for the functionalist to maintain that qualia don't matter in this case. It seems that, if there are no qualia at all when my twin is in pain, then he isn't really in pain or, indeed, in any mental state at all. If this hypothesis is coherent, then functionalism is in trouble, for we have another reason for thinking that a mental state like pain cannot be a mere functional state. In addition to its functional properties, for something to be a sensation it also requires some kind of qualitative character. Although we have seen that there is reason to be sceptical of the idea that there is one quale common to all sensations of a given kind, it seems as though a sensation ought to feel like *something*. If the functionalist denies this, then functionalism seems very implausible.

The possibility of beings like zombies is highly disputed. Defenders of functionalism often claim that zombies are not really possible, in which case they cannot be used to undermine functionalism. One reason for thinking zombies are impossible is that the very idea is incoherent in some way. Some critics point out that it makes no sense to talk about zombies because we are being asked to imagine the existence of something that would be impossible to detect. That is, since zombies are indistinguishable from the rest of us, we could never have any empirical reasons for thinking someone is a zombie, and without some means of distinguishing zombies from conscious beings, it is difficult to see why we should take the idea of a zombie seriously.

Another potential problem with the absent qualia argument is that it treats the idea of functional equivalence between me and my zombie twin too loosely. When critics of functionalism invoke the concept of a zombie, the tendency is to focus on the observable, behavioural aspects of functional states. For instance, they speak only of the causes of pain (bodily damage) and its bodily effects (withdrawal from the stimulus and verbal behaviour). However, as we saw, functionalists think that a proper functional analysis of a mental state like pain should include some reference to other mental states as well. In addition to a withdrawal reflex and verbal complaints, pain causes fear, anxiety, and dislike. If my zombie twin were truly functionally equivalent to me, then it must also feel fear, anxiety, and dislike. In this case, though, we need to abandon the idea that my twin is a zombie, for if a being feels fear and anxiety, it has qualitative states of consciousness. Zombies are supposed to lack qualia by definition, so anything with qualia cannot be a zombie. It seems that a being that is truly functionally identical to a conscious creature (and not merely behaviourally indistinguishable) must also be conscious, in which case critics of functionalism cannot employ zombies to make their case, for zombies are behaviourally, not functionally, identical to conscious creatures like ourselves.

Despite its problems, functionalism is probably the most widely accepted theory of mind among philosophers today and has given rise to some fascinating and productive research in cognitive science and artificial intelligence. Its critics maintain that qualia represent a stubborn obstacle to the functional account of mental states like sensations because the functional analysis of a sensation like pain does not appear to capture the painfulness of pain. This is an issue we will revisit in Chapter 9. Functionalism emerged as a theory of mind largely in response to pressures put on the type identity theory by neural plasticity and multiple realization. In the next chapter we will explore an alternative reaction to these problems.

Suggestions for Further Reading

Block, N. 1980. "Troubles with Functionalism." *Readings in Philosophy of Psychology*. Vol. 1. N. Block. Cambridge, MA.: Harvard University Press.

Churchland, P., and P. Churchland. 1981. "Functionalism, Qualia, and Intentionality." *Philosophical Topics* 12: 121–46.

Putnam, H. 1964. "Robots: Machines or Artificially Created Life?" *Journal of Philosophy* 61: 691–94.

Putnam, H. 1971. "The Nature of Mental States." *Materialism and the Mind-Body Problem*. Ed. David Rosenthal. Englewood Cliffs, NJ: Prentice-Hall.

Shoemaker, S. 1982. "The Inverted Spectrum." *Journal of Philosophy* 79: 357–81.

CHAPTER 5

■ ANOMALOUS MONISM

Historical Influences

In Chapter 3 we saw that the type identity theory encountered serious philosophical problems in light of the principle of multiple realization. According to the principle of multiple realization, it is possible for physically diverse creatures to have mental states of the same kind. This possibility is at odds with the reductive approach taken by type identity theorists who assert that a type of mental state such as pain can be reduced to, or is *nothing more* than, a type of brain state such as the firing of C-fibres. However, if a silicon-based life form without C-fibres can feel pain, this seems to preclude the identity theorist's reductive strategy, for then it turns out that there is no one kind of physical state to which pain can be reduced. In light of this, materialists required an alternative way of understanding how mental states could be physical states.

Because of the incompatibility between multiple realization on the one hand and the aim to reduce mental states to physical states on the other, several philosophers have proposed that we should develop a form of physicalism that is *non-reductive*. The first of these non-reductive theories was functionalism, which we explored in detail in the previous chapter. Functionalists recommended that we think of mental states not in terms of their *intrinsic* physical properties (what they are made of) as the type identity theorists did, but in terms of their *extrinsic* relational properties (their causal roles). Since these causal roles can be realized in a variety of different ways by diverse kinds of physical materials, functionalists deny the reductive claim that mental states are *nothing more* than brain states. Despite being non-reductive, functionalism remains a form of physicalism because it claims that physical stuff is probably the only kind of material capable of realizing the causal roles that define mental states; multiple realization requires only that there is *more than one* kind of physical stuff that is able to do this.

A second form of non-reductive materialism is **anomalous monism**, developed by Donald Davidson. At the centre of Davidson's discussion of the relationship between the mental and the physical is the concept of an **event**—an occurrence or happening. My feeling pain when I stubbed my toe yesterday and the assassination of the Archduke Franz Ferdinand are both examples of events. For Davidson, events are token occurrences; they are unique occurrences because the same event cannot happen more than once. I cannot feel the *same* pain that I did yesterday even if I stub my toe repeatedly. At best, I can have a series of distinct sensations which are similar to the pain

I felt yesterday. All these pains are sensations of the same kind (pain), but they are all unique, unrepeatable token occurrences. Likewise, the assassination of Ferdinand can happen only once. There can be many *attempts* at assassination, but even those are token events that cannot be repeated since each assassination attempt is unique.

One of the interesting things about events is that we can describe the same event in different ways by identifying the same event but using different words to do so. When we do this, we consider the same event under **alternative descriptions**. For instance, the assassination of the Archduke Franz Ferdinand can be variously described as:

1. The event that occurred in Sarajevo on June 28, 1914.
2. The event that started World War I.
3. The assassination of the heir to the Austro-Hungarian throne.

Each of these descriptions picks out the same event and so are alternative descriptions of the very same occurrence. All of them pick out Ferdinand's assassination in a way that is fairly general, and none provide much detail about the event in question. Presumably, however, there are more precise descriptions of this event that capture the more fine-grained details of the occurrence, including the angle and velocity of the bullet, the trajectory it took through Ferdinand's body, the precise cause of death, and so on. In fact, we can even suppose that there is a description of this event in terms of the relative position of each atom that made up the Archduke's body, the bullet, the gun, etc. Of course, we could never formulate such a description since it would doubtless be extremely long and complicated, but *in principle* there is a way to describe this event using the vocabulary of the most basic physical theory. So let's add to our list of descriptions the following:

4. The event with such and such atomic characteristics.

Davidson would suggest that descriptions (1)-(4) are all descriptions of the same kind; the difference between them is merely one of degree. That is, each one describes the event in question as a physical occurrence, but (4) identifies the event in question at a more precise level of physical description than (1)-(3) because it picks out more details. Hence, (1)-(4) are all **physical descriptions**.

In addition to these physical descriptions it is also possible to pick out Ferdinand's assassination under a **mental description** as:

5. The event Gavrilo Princip believed would free his people from Austro-Hungarian rule.

This is a mental description because it employs **psychological vocabulary**, in this case the word "belief." According to Davidson, then, the same event can have both a mental and a physical description. An event is a *mental event* when it is picked out under a mental description (i.e., one that employs psychological terms or concepts such as *belief, sensation, thought, desire*, etc.). Similarly, an event is a *physical event* when it is picked out under a physical description (i.e., one that employs physical vocabulary such as the terms of physical theory or the language of ordinary, everyday objects).

Davidson claims that our mental states, such as the having of sensations, beliefs, desires, and the like, are occurrences and are thus best thought-of as mental events. Since *all* events have alternative descriptions, our mental events have alternative descriptions too. Just as the event of Ferdinand's assassination has an alternative *mental description*, Davidson claims our having thoughts and sensations are events that have alternative *physical descriptions*. For example, my feeling pain is an event. When I say that I feel pain, I am picking out that event under a mental description because I am using mental vocabulary to describe it. However, this event also has a physical description, presumably in neurological terms. This means that mental events are not a special class of things distinct from physical events that need to be housed in a non-physical mind or soul. They are simply physical events described using the vocabulary of psychology. Because Davidson does not endorse the existence of mental substances or non-physical states, his theory is a form of physicalism. Physicalism, of course, is a form of monism in contrast to dualism, because it claims that there is only one kind of stuff in the world: physical stuff.

Because Davidson thinks mental events are physical events described in psychological terms, **anomalous monism** is a form of identity theory, but it is quite different from the identity theories of Smart and Place we explored earlier. Those theories were *type* identity theories, whereas Davidson's is a *token* identity theory. A type identity theory attempts to identify mental types (e.g., pain) with physical types (e.g., the firing of C-fibres). Davidson clearly rejects this idea with his proposal that we should identify mental tokens with physical tokens. On this view, my token pain (the one I felt when I stubbed my toe yesterday) is identical to a token physical event in my central nervous system, which is why my sensation has a physical description in addition to its mental description. Just as each occurrence of pain is unique, so too is each physical event with which those token pains are identical. Thus, the next time I stub my toe, the pain I will feel will be identical to a distinct physical event.

Davidson's brand of identity theory is consistent with the possibilities that were such a problem for the type identity theory. First, token identity allows for radically different species to have the same kinds of mental states. For instance, suppose that Marvin, my silicon friend from another planet, and I can both feel sensations of pain. Imagine that we both suffer some kind of bodily injury at the same time. At that moment we both have the same *kind* or *type* of experience since we both feel pain. However, we each experience distinct *token* sensations. The pain I feel is a mental event that is distinct from Marvin's. I cannot feel Marvin's pain and Marvin cannot feel mine. According to Davidson, my token pain is identical to an unrepeatable token event in my body, such as the firing of a particular set of neurons in a particular way. Marvin's token pain is identical to a token event in his body, presumably a silicon event that is also unrepeatable. Thus, my pain and Marvin's pain are both identical to physical events, but my pain is identical to a different physical event than Marvin's pain. Since my pain and Marvin's pain are distinct physical events, pain cannot be reduced to one kind of physical state, such as a brain state. The type identity theory is not consistent with this possibility, but the token identity theory is, in which case it is on a better philosophical footing, provided we take the possibility of multiple realization seriously in the first place.

Davidson's approach is also consistent with the possibility of neural plasticity. Since my token pains are identical to token physical events, it is not necessary for my brain to be in the same kind of state every time I have the same kind or type of sensation. The pain that I felt when I broke my arm at age eight was identical with a neural event, but the one I felt yesterday when I stubbed my toe is identical to a distinct neural event that could be quite different from the earlier one. Davidson's approach requires only that each token pain be identical with a token physical event. Those physical events need not be events of the same kind, just as my pain and Marvin's pain are different kinds of physical events. Thus, Davidson's approach is consistent with the possibility that a different part of the brain might take over the processing of painful stimuli if the part of the brain that used to do it were damaged at some point.

Davidson's Three Claims

Davidson develops his theory by trying to reconcile the following three claims, which appear to be in conflict:

1. At least some mental events enter causal relations with physical events.
2. Events related as cause and effect fall under strict deterministic laws.
3. There are no strict psychophysical laws.

The first claim seems to be true on the basis of our everyday experiences. Every time we perform an intentional action, our deciding or choosing (which are both mental events) causes our physical behaviour (the intended action). Similarly, physical events in the world seem to cause mental events, as when the impact of my toe against the leg of the coffee table causes a sensation of pain. Thus, this first claim seems to be fairly innocuous.

The second claim has its origins in the work of Galileo and Newton and is generally accepted by philosophers of science. We have already seen something like this idea in Chapter 1. It involves a model of the universe as a closed system according to which every event that occurs does so in accordance with universal laws of nature. On this view, whenever there is a causal relationship between two events, this relationship is governed by one or more of these universal laws. For instance, if I have a balloon with air in it and squeeze it so that I decrease its volume, the air pressure inside the balloon increases. Here I am describing a causal relationship between two events: my decreasing the volume of the balloon is the cause, and the effect is the increasing of the pressure inside the balloon. The described effect is not something that happens just by chance; it happens because there is a law of nature, called Boyle's Law, connecting the pressure of a gas with its volume. Boyle's Law is an example of a **strict deterministic law**, a law that does not admit exceptions. The pressure of a gas isn't connected with its volume *sometimes*, or *most of the time*; it is *always* connected. To say that a cause and an effect "fall under" a strict deterministic law (or that such a law "covers" a given causal relationship) is to say that some such law governs the relationship between them and determines the outcome of the cause. In this example, the cause and the effect are said to fall under Boyle's Law since that is the law that determines the result. What Davidson is saying in his second claim is that *all* causal relationships are like this. Wherever there are causes and effects, there are strict laws.

The third claim denies that there can be strict laws connecting mental events and physical events. This is obviously in tension with the first two claims, for if Davidson believes that mental events enter causal relationships with physical events, and that events related as cause and effect fall under strict deterministic laws, then it would seem to follow that there are strict deterministic laws connecting mental events with physical events (i.e., *psychophysical* laws). It is Davidson's denial of psychophysical laws that leads him to call his view *anomalous monism*. To be anomalous is to escape capture in the net of universal laws of nature that determine the way the world works. By denying that there are strict psychophysical laws, Davidson is saying that the mental is anomalous. His task, then, is to reconcile these three principles and to relieve the tension between them while remaining committed to their truth. He tries to achieve this by clarifying the meaning of the second claim and by offering further justification for the third claim.

Singular Causal Claims and Causal Laws

In clarifying his second claim, Davidson argues that there is an important difference between causation, singular causal claims, and causal laws. Causation, Davidson claims, is a relationship that holds between events in the world independently of the way we describe them or even of our noticing them. For example, he would say that the shining of the sun causes the warming of a particular grain of sand in the middle of the Sahara Desert whether anyone knows it or not. Singular causal claims, however, depend on us because they are statements or assertions we make when we say that one event caused another. To take one of Davidson's own examples (modified slightly), let's suppose that a hurricane that swept through the area on Tuesday caused the collapse of a bridge on Wednesday. We might offer the following singular causal claim:

1. The hurricane caused the collapse of a bridge.

All singular causal claims pick out the cause and the effect *under a description.* That is, the cause and the effect each have to be described in some way or other when we make causal claims, otherwise we wouldn't know which causes and effects we were talking about. In this case the cause was described as *the hurricane*, and the effect was described as *the collapse of a bridge.*

We have already seen that there are many different ways in which we can describe the same event. Thus, there are many different ways in which one can formulate this singular causal claim. All we need to do is pick out the cause and the effect under different true descriptions. Suppose, then, that the hurricane was reported on the front page of the newspaper on Wednesday and that the collapse of the bridge was reported on the front page of the newspaper on Thursday. We could then offer the following true singular causal claim:

2. The event reported on the front page of Wednesday's paper caused the event reported on the front page of Thursday's paper.

This is considerably less informative than the first version of our causal claim, but is no less true because of it. As with the assassination of Ferdinand, the events can also, presumably, be picked out at an extremely detailed level of description in terms of velocities, forces, and the like. If we were to fill in the variables appropriately to provide these detailed descriptions, we could also express our singular causal claim as follows:

3. The event with forces of velocity x caused the event with forces of velocity y.

We now have three alternative formulations of our singular causal claim. They are all true, and all refer to the same cause and the same effect. Of course, many other descriptions of the cause and the effect are possible, which would yield even more ways of expressing the causal claim, but these three will suffice for our purposes.

Davidson has said that every causal relation falls under a strict causal law. What is the law that covers *this* causal relation? We saw above that one way of describing the causal relationship between the hurricane and the collapse of a bridge was in terms of newspaper headlines (*the event reported on the front page of Wednesday's paper caused the event reported on the front page of Thursday's paper*). Does this mean that there is a strict deterministic law connecting newspaper headlines? Obviously not; it would be absurd to think that there could be such a law since the newspaper headlines vary daily.

We also expressed the causal claim in terms of hurricanes and collapsing bridges (*The hurricane caused the collapse of a bridge*). Perhaps there is a strict law connecting hurricanes and the collapsing of bridges? While it is not obvious that there isn't such a law, it would seem very implausible to suggest that there is. Hurricanes tend to be destructive, so they often cause events like the collapse of bridges or the destruction of homes, but this is only a generalization and not a strict law. Generalizations are *often* true, whereas strict laws are *always* true. If there were a strict law connecting hurricanes and the collapsing of bridges, the former would *always* cause the latter, without exception. Clearly this is not the case since bridges don't collapse every time there is a hurricane. If neither of these two singular causal claims involves laws, then what does this mean for Davidson's assertion that wherever there is a causal relationship there is a strict causal law? Do these considerations show that his claim is false?

The fact that we can't formulate a strict law in terms of either newspaper headlines or of hurricanes and the collapsing of bridges *does not* mean that a strict law does not cover this causal relationship. What it *does* show is that the strict law that covers a given causal relationship does not necessarily employ the same concepts or vocabulary as the singular causal claim. That is, we might be able to express the relevant law only when we employ different descriptions of the cause and the effect than the ones used in the singular causal claim. Our third formulation of the causal claim (*The event with forces of velocity x caused the event with forces of velocity y*) employs a much more precise vocabulary than either of the other two formulations, and we find it easy to imagine that there is a strict deterministic law between the events when described in this way because there is a connection between being a candidate for a strict law and being a fine-grained physical description of a cause and an effect. Strict laws require very detailed and precise descriptions. There is no law connecting an object's being heavy with its velocity, but there is a law connecting an object's mass with its velocity. Being a hurricane or a newspaper headline is like being heavy; it is too rough or imprecise to figure in a law of nature.

The significance of all this is that it provides a way for Davidson to reconcile his three claims. Suppose that my having a sensation of pain causes me to utter "Ouch!" Here we have a singular causal claim to the effect that a mental event caused a physical event:

My sensing pain caused my uttering "Ouch!"

Naturally, these events have been picked out under a description. The cause has been described as *my sensing pain*, which is a mental description, and the effect has been described as *my uttering "Ouch!"* which is a physical description. According to Davidson, this causal relation is backed by a strict causal law. However, the lesson we learned from our discussion of the hurricane and the collapsing bridge is that the law at work in any causal relationship does not always employ the same descriptions of events as those employed in the singular causal claim. Thus, it might be that the law connecting my sensing pain with my utterance uses different descriptions of these events. Davidson has proposed that mental events are identical to physical events, in which case there must be an alternative, physical description of my sensing pain in neurological (or even atomic) terms. Furthermore, there must be a more detailed physical description of my utterance in terms of physiological processes (or even in terms of configurations of atoms). In Davidson's view it is *these* descriptions of the cause and the effect that will figure in the relevant strict law, but then the law uses only *physical terms or concepts.*

Davidson therefore reconciles his three claims in the following way. Mental events do indeed have causal interaction with physical events. However, mental events are token identical to physical events, and so have physical descriptions. The laws that connect mental causes with physical effects (or vice versa) make use of very detailed physical descriptions of the cause and of the effect. Thus, there are only strict physical laws, not psychophysical laws.

Laws of Nature and Psychological Vocabulary

The previous section explains how it is possible for mental and physical events to enter into causal relationships without generating psychophysical laws, but it is still unclear why psychophysical laws are *impossible.* To understand this, we need to appreciate in more detail the difference between laws and generalizations and the difference between physical and mental descriptions.

We have seen one reason for denying the possibility of psychophysical (or psychological) laws: that mental descriptions of events are too rough and imprecise to be suited to the formulation of strict laws. Let's look more closely at why this is the case. Mental events figure prominently in a variety of generalizations about human behaviour. For instance, we say that people who feel pain tend to wince, that people who feel thirsty tend to drink water if it is handy, and so on. These generalizations are true, but they are far from being strict laws. Even though most people wince when they feel pain, not all of them do. Some people have a very high threshold for pain, and others have trained themselves not to exhibit behavioural reactions to painful sensations. Similarly, even though most people who are thirsty will drink water that is given to them, they will only drink it if they believe it isn't poisoned, or if they don't dislike the taste of water and would prefer to wait for a different drink. Every psychological generalization one can think of is subject to these kinds of exceptions. Strict laws admit of no exceptions at all, in which case it is inappropriate to think of these generalizations as though they were laws. Since the best candidates we have for psychophysical laws fall well short of the mark, there is good reason to be sceptical of the possibility of strict psychophysical laws. These concerns are further enforced by the difference in the relative precision of our physical vocabulary and our mental vocabulary.

As we have already seen, not all physical descriptions of events are amenable to the formulation of strict laws. Some are simply too vague or imprecise. For instance, *hurricane* is a physical description of an event, but it is not the kind of description we are likely to encounter in a strict law. Similarly, *fast* is a physical description of an event, but it is doubtful that there are any strict laws that use it. These kinds of physical descriptions, however, can be sharpened into greater detail while still using physical vocabulary; instead of talking about a hurricane, we might talk about certain forces travelling along particular vectors, and instead of talking about something being fast, we might speak about its velocity. These kinds of descriptions *do* figure in strict laws. In the end, our physical descriptions yield the kind of detailed and determinate descriptions of events that are required for strict laws and that were absent from our initially vague and indeterminate descriptions. The problem with our mental descriptions is that they are *essentially* vague and indeterminate. The reason our mental descriptions are too vague to play a role in strict laws is, according to Davidson, due largely to the **normativity** of our psychological vocabulary.

Davidson claims that we ascribe mental states to one another and to ourselves in the process of trying to predict and explain behaviour. Suppose that we are talking, and I say "Boy, it's bright out," and I close the blinds. You will probably attribute a certain set of beliefs and desires to me including (but not limited to) the following: I was *bothered* by the light coming in through the window; I had a *desire* to make the room darker; and I *believed* that closing the blinds would make the room darker. What has happened here is that you have taken an event (the cause of my closing the blinds) and described it using mental vocabulary. The reason you attribute to me the various mental states you do is that you are guided by a principle that Davidson calls the **normativity of rationality**, which requires you to preserve my rationality. That is, the reason you think I have these mental states is because by assuming I do, my closing the blinds is a *rational* action. Thus, attributing these mental states to me preserves my rationality.

Suppose that a little later in the conversation, I start peeking nervously through the blinds and tell you that I believe some-one has been following me. In light of this, you are likely to re-evaluate the mental ascriptions you made earlier and to ascribe a different set of mental states to me, including (but not limited to) the following: I am *afraid* that someone might be watching me through the window; I have a *desire* to conceal myself; I *believe* that drawing the blinds will hide me from my pursuer. Once again, the guiding principle that determines which mental states you ascribe to me is normativity: you are attempt-ing to make sense of my behaviour in a way that preserves my status as a rational being. If one believes one is being followed, it is rational to want to hide and to do what is necessary (under the circumstances) to achieve that aim.

Davidson's view is that this process is a never-ending one; we are constantly revisiting and altering our mental ascriptions in the light of new episodes of behaviour. This is why mental descriptions of events are ill-suited to the formulation of strict laws. When we measure the velocity of an object at a particu-lar time this fact is determined once and for all. If an object was travelling at 10 metres per second at time *t* we do not revisit this fact in light of what happens later. However, when we describe an event as a belief the content of that belief is likely to change over time as we try to preserve the rationality of the agent in the light of new behaviour. Mental descriptions, then, are indeterminate in a way that physical descriptions are not. Since strict laws describe the way things must behave, without exception, strict laws require descriptions of events that are fixed and determinate, not descriptions that are liable to change radically over time. This precludes the possibility of strict psychophysical laws.

Anomalous Monism and Epiphenomenalism

Anomalous monism has come under tremendous criticism. The objection most philosophers have raised is that anomalous monism leads to a form of epiphenomenalism. In Chapter 1 we saw that epiphenomenalism is the view that, contrary to how things seem, our mental states do not cause anything, not even our behaviour. This is somewhat different from the form of epiphenomenalism Davidson's critics accuse him of holding. They do not think Davidson's views have the implication that mental *events* are epiphenomenal, but that mental *properties* are.

At the heart of the objection is the idea that when one event causes another, it does so only in virtue of some of its properties. For example, suppose I drop a brick on to a glass coffee table and that the impact of the brick against the glass causes the glass to shatter. The brick has certain properties at the moment it comes into contact with the glass: it has a certain density and it is travelling at a certain velocity and in a certain direction. But these are not the only properties the brick has. It is also orange, and I often use it as a paperweight. Do all of these properties contribute to what happens when the brick strikes the glass, or do some of these properties matter more than others? It seems fairly clear the first set of properties I mentioned contribute significantly to the effect. If the brick had not been dense, travelling at that velocity and in that direction, the effect might not have occurred—the glass might not have broken. As such, we should say that the first set of properties is **causally efficacious**, that is, they make a causal contribution to the production of the effect. The second set of properties seems different. The fact I use that brick as a paperweight or that it is orange as opposed to some other colour does not appear to contribute to the breaking of the glass. If the brick were some other colour and were never used by me as a paperweight, it would presumably have broken the glass just the same. Since these properties do not contribute to the production of the effect, they are **epiphenomenal**.

To say that the colour of the brick and the fact I use it as a paperweight are epiphenomenal is not to say that these properties don't cause *anything*. They do have effects of their own. For instance, the colour of the brick causes me to say that it is orange rather than blue, and the fact I use the brick as a paperweight causes my papers to remain on my desk. These properties, then, are epiphenomenal only in a limited sense. They are epiphenomenal *with respect to a particular effect*—in this case, the breaking of the coffee table.

It is interesting to note that the properties of the brick that are causally relevant in this context are just those properties that would figure in the strict law that covers this causal relationship. Thus, it would seem that events cause what they do in virtue of the properties mentioned in strict laws and not in virtue of any other properties.

These ideas become very significant in cases where mental events enter into causal relationships with physical events. We saw that Davidson accepts the claim that in order to formulate the strict law covering such relations we must employ physical descriptions of the cause and the effect. Let's draw on our previous example to clarify matters here. We said that the mental event of my sensing pain caused the physical event of my utterance. According to Davidson, this causal claim is backed by a strict law, but that law does not employ the existing descriptions of these events. Instead, the law probably uses a neurological description of the cause and a physiological description of the effect. This seems to be analogous to the example of the brick breaking the glass. Just as the impact of the brick caused the shattering of the glass only in virtue of certain properties of the cause (the density, velocity, and trajectory of the brick), my sensing pain caused my behaviour only in virtue of the neurological properties of my pain. Furthermore, just as certain properties of the brick were epiphenomenal with respect to the shattering of the glass, certain properties of my pain seem to be epiphenomenal with respect to my utterance. In this case, the epiphenomenal properties are the ones we picked out in our initial mental description of the cause: all the mental properties of the event, such as the painfulness of my sensation.

The full significance of this becomes apparent only when we see how this line of reasoning generalizes to all mental events. When I decide to perform an action and then do it, we ordinarily think my deciding is what causes my action. According to the argument above, this is not strictly true. What really causes my action are the physical properties of the event that is my deciding, such as the fact that my neurons fired in a particular configuration, and not the mental properties of that event, such as the fact that I decided, or desired, to perform that action. We ordinarily think that many of our actions are the result of the fact that we have the beliefs and desires we do. Davidson's view seems to deny this, for the real causal work is not done by the fact that our beliefs and desires are the particular beliefs and desires they are, but by the fact that our bodies are in a particular physical state. Because most philosophers think that the mental properties of our beliefs, desires, and choices matter to our behaviour, they find the version of epiphenomenalism entailed by Davidson's theory to be very unappealing, for it seems to strip us of any genuine rational agency and to turn us into the hapless victims of physical processes.

Davidson has tried to defend anomalous monism from this objection, but most of his critics seem to think that the objection is unavoidable. Despite these difficulties, Davidson's views have been extremely influential. In addition to token identity, he also introduced the idea that the mental *supervenes* on the physical. We will examine the concept of supervenience in Chapter 7.

Suggestions for Further Reading

Davidson, D. 1970. "Mental Events." *Experience and Theory*. Ed. L. Foster and J. Swanson. Amherst, MA: University of Massachusetts Press.

Davidson, D. 1993. "Thinking Causes." *Mental Causation*. Ed. J. Heil and A. Mele. Oxford: Clarendon Press.

Honderich, T. 1982. "The Argument for Anomalous Monism." *Analysis* 42: 59–64.

Honderich, T. 1983. "Anomalous Monism: Reply to Smith." *Analysis* 43: 147–49.

Honderich, T. 1984. "Smith and the Champion of Mauve." *Analysis* 44: 86–89.

Kim, J. 1993. "Can Supervenience and 'Non-Strict Laws' Save Anomalous Monism?" *Mental Causation*. Ed. J. Heil and A. Mele. Oxford: Clarendon.

LePore, E., and B.P. McLaughlin. 1985. *Actions and Events: Perspectives on the Philosophy of Donald Davidson*. Oxford: Blackwell.

Smith, P. 1982. "Bad News for Anomalous Monism." *Analysis* 42: 220–24.

Smith, P. 1984. "Anomalous Monism and Epiphenomenalism: A Reply to Honderich." *Analysis* 41: 83–86.

CHAPTER 6

ELIMINATIVE MATERIALISM

Theoretical Elimination

To this point we have examined a number of different versions of physicalism, most of which react to Cartesian dualism in the same way: they identify mental states with physical states. Behaviourists identify mental states with behavioural dispositions; type identity theorists identify mental states with types of brain states; token identity theorists identify them with token physical events; and functionalists identify them with functional states that are physically realized. Eliminative materialists claim that all these theories take the wrong approach. We should not try to identify mental states with physical states; instead, we should learn to appreciate that there are no such things as mental states at all. We should *eliminate* mental states from our ontology.

Our ontology is the catalogue of all the things we believe actually exist in the universe. To eliminate something from our ontology is therefore to deny its existence. By way of illustration, eliminative materialists often point to historically successful cases of elimination, such as the concept of **caloric**. Caloric is a substance that was posited to explain the thermal behaviour of material bodies. We routinely observe that objects can change temperature. For example, when we put a wet pair of shoes next to a fire, the shoes warm up, and when the shoes are removed from the presence of the fire, they cool down again. Prior to the seventeenth century, scientists proposed that heat was an invisible fluid called caloric, and they developed caloric theory to explain the thermal behaviour of bodies in terms of the flow of caloric from one body to another. They claimed that caloric flowed from the fire to the shoes and then seeped out of the shoes later on when they were removed from the presence of the fire. Then scientists developed a new and competing account of heat, according to which the temperature of a body is just the kinetic energy of the molecules that make it up. So what happened to caloric? Was it reduced to molecular kinetic energy? No. Caloric was not reduced but *eliminated*; that is, scientists did not identify caloric with molecular kinetic energy, they concluded that caloric does not exist. According to the kinetic theory of heat, temperature is a state of excitation of the molecules that make up objects. When an object heats up or cools down, this is due only to a change in the level of excitation of the object's molecules. Thus, heat is not something that travels in and out of objects, for heat is not itself a *substance* or *thing*. In light of this, there was no longer any need for caloric, so it was eliminated.

Let's consider a second example. Before the Copernican revolution, many people believed the Earth was the centre of the universe and that the celestial bodies of the night sky were embedded in a series of concentric crystal spheres that revolved at different velocities around our planet. Those who accepted this picture would look up at the night sky and say that they could literally see the spheres of the heavens turning. Now we have a completely different understanding of the universe: our planet and solar system are located on the periphery of one of many spiral arms of one of many galaxies. We know that the stars are not embedded in crystal spheres and that it was a mistake ever to think there were such things. The crystal spheres of the heavens were consequently eliminated as an unnecessary, mistaken, and misleading part of the furniture of the universe.

Eliminative materialists (e.g., Paul and Patricia Churchland) think that mental states are part of a primitive theory of human behaviour called **folk psychology**. That is, our commonsense psychological framework, according to which human beings have mental states like beliefs, desires, and sensations, is literally a theory that we all use to predict and explain one another's behaviour. The difference between folk psychology and other theories is that folk psychology is adopted by ordinary people rather than by scientists and is learned as we grow up. As such, we tend not to think of it as a theory; since it has become such an integral and seemingly natural part of our way of dealing with one another, we overlook its theoretical status. Eliminative materialists claim that, as natural and indispensable as it seems, folk psychology is actually a false and misleading account of the causes of human behaviour. Just as caloric was eliminated when people realized that caloric theory is false, and just as the spheres of the heavens were eliminated when the geocentric model of the universe was abandoned, so too mental states will be eliminated when we realize that folk psychology is false. Furthermore, just as caloric theory and the geocentric theory of the universe were replaced by better theories, folk psychology will be replaced by a mature neuroscience.

Now that we understand the broad strokes of eliminative materialism, what reasons are there to support this view? To understand these we need to appreciate why some philosophers think folk psychology is a theory.

Why Folk Psychology is a Theory

The first reason for thinking folk psychology is a theory is that it serves the same general purpose as all theories. Among other things, theories are predictive-explanatory frameworks. We use theories to provide explanations of phenomena and to predict future events. For example, the theory of gravitation provides us with an explanation of the trajectory of Halley's Comet and allows us to predict its location over long periods of time. Folk psychology also provides us with an explanatory framework since it allows us to predict and explain *human* behaviour. Our usual method of explaining the behaviour of human beings is by identifying their mental states. We talk about what they believe, desire, or how they felt at the time they acted, and doing so seems to explain their actions admirably. For instance, saying that I wanted to dim the light is usually a perfectly good explanation for why I pulled down the blinds. Similarly, knowing that I want to dim the light before I act is likely to yield the true prediction that I will pull down the blinds. Thus, at this level folk psychology does resemble a theory.

Aside from these rather general similarities there are two other grounds for thinking folk psychology is a theory. First, there is reason to believe that mental states are theoretical entities that get their meaning in the same way as the entities posited by *any* theory. Consider atomic theory. It consists of a set of laws that specify a set of relations between various entities and observable facts. For instance, it postulates such things as protons, neutrons, and electrons and states how these things are related to one another. In order to understand the terms "proton," "neutron," and "electron" we need to understand the role of these concepts within atomic theory. That is, unless one has some understanding of the theory as a whole and of the relationship between protons, neutrons, and electrons, one cannot really understand what these words mean. Such terms, then, are implicitly defined by the network of principles and relations in which they figure. One of the most outspoken eliminative materialists, Paul Churchland, calls this the **network theory of meaning** and claims that all theoretical entities derive their meaning in this way.

According to Churchland, the network theory of meaning is also true of our mental vocabulary. Mental terms like "belief," "desire," "sensation," and so on derive their meanings in the same way as words like "proton." To see this we need first to recognize that folk psychology is in large part constituted by a set of generalizations that function much like the laws of other theories. Here are several examples of folk psychological generalizations: *people who suffer recent bodily damage tend to feel pain; people who feel pain tend to say "Ouch"; people who feel hungry tend to eat; people who believe x tend to act in a way that is consistent with that belief; if people desire x and it is within their ability to achieve x, they will do what they believe is necessary to achieve x.* On Churchland's view, the place of beliefs, desires, and other mental concepts within generalizations of this sort constitutes our understanding of these concepts. For instance, in order to understand what a belief is, one needs to understand its relationship to intentional actions and its relationship to other mental states like desire, knowledge, doubt, and so on. Since our mental terms are defined by the network theory of meaning, and since this is how all theoretical terms are defined, our mental terms are probably theoretical terms.

A second reason for thinking folk psychology is a theory is that the explanations and predictions afforded to us by our psychological framework function in the same way as the explanations provided by scientific theories generally. Suppose I watched a hot air balloon expanding in preparation for take-off, and I ask my companion, "Why did the balloon expand?" She might respond by saying, "Because they heated up the air inside the balloon." Usually this would suffice, but suppose I insist on a fuller explanation. My companion might then offer the following:

> All gases expand when heated.
> This balloon is filled with a gas.
> The gas was heated.
> Therefore, this balloon expanded.

Churchland says that scientific explanations usually take this form, that of a deductive argument whose premises (the

explanans) consist of at least one law plus a statement of the initial conditions. The conclusion of the argument is the fact that needs explaining (the **explanandum**). The explanation itself consists in our being able to deduce the fact we wanted to explain from the law and initial conditions. If the explanandum did not follow from the premises, we would not have explained anything. Because this pattern of explanation takes the form of a deductive argument and uses laws in the premises, these explanations are called **deductive nomological (DN) explanations** (the word "nomological" means "lawlike").

The same pattern of relationships also allows us to make predictions. All we need to do is restate the relevant premises and the conclusion in the future tense:

> All gases expand when heated.
> This balloon is filled with a gas.
> This gas will be heated.
> Therefore, this balloon will expand.

Again, our prediction consists in our deducing the prediction from the statement of the initial conditions and the relevant law. Ordinarily, we do not bother to make our explanations or predictions this explicit. Most of the time a partial account is enough. For instance, being told that the air in the balloon was heated is usually enough to explain why the balloon expanded, but this is true only because the other premises in the argument are assumed in the background. That is, to reply to my question "Why did the balloon expand?" by saying "Because the air inside was heated" is satisfactory because we can assume

I know that balloons contain gas and that gases expand when heated. Only if someone were ignorant of these other facts would anyone be tempted to formulate an explanation as explicit as the one above.

Churchland claims that our folk psychological explanations and predictions of human behaviour also follow the DN model. In the place of laws, however, we employ the kind of folk psychological generalizations mentioned above. For example, suppose Don suddenly utters "Ouch." I could offer the following explanation for this fact:

> People who suffer recent bodily damage tend to feel pain.
> People who feel pain tend to say "Ouch."
> I damaged Don's finger.
> Therefore, Don said "Ouch."

Once again, our explanation takes the form of a deductive argument with the explanandum as the conclusion, but this time folk psychological generalizations play the role of laws in the premises. It seems, then, that our commonsense explanations of human behaviour bear a strong resemblance to DN explanations, but what about *predictions* of human behaviour? We can see that folk psychological predictions work in the same way as scientific predictions by adjusting this argument in the same way we adjusted the previous one.

> People who suffer recent bodily damage tend to feel pain.
> People who feel pain tend to say "Ouch."
> I will damage Don's finger.
> Therefore, Don will say "Ouch."

We can see from this that our predictions of human behaviour also follow the DN model, for the prediction is deduced from a set of laws and initial conditions. Of course, we seldom bother to make our folk psychological explanations or predictions so explicit, because we can assume the presence and role of folk psychological generalizations like the two above in the background. We all know that people who suffer recent bodily damage tend to feel pain and that people who feel pain tend to say "Ouch," so it is usually unnecessary to point this out when we predict or explain behaviour like Don's. What we have seen, then, is that there is a tremendous parallel in the structure of folk psychological explanations and predictions and those of scientific theories. Since all these predictions and explanations follow the DN model, we have another reason to believe that folk psychology is a theory.

We will see below that there is considerable room for disagreement about these claims. For now, however, there do seem to be a number of similarities between folk psychology and scientific theories. In light of these similarities, it is reasonable to conclude that folk psychology is a theory.

The Introspection of Mental States

One might think the eliminative materialist's claim that folk psychology is a theory is plausible when it comes to predicting and explaining the behaviour of others, but it is very implausible in one's own case. Since the mental states of others are unobservable, it makes a certain amount of sense to treat those states as theoretical entities that we posit to understand the behaviour of those around us. However, you likely think your relationship to your own mental states is entirely different, that you know your own mental states directly. Your beliefs and desires might be inaccessible to others, but you have a special privileged access to your own mind. All you need to do is look inward, to introspect, to see that your mental states are as real as anything can be. In light of this, it probably seems very implausible—if not absurd—to think that mental states could be mere theoretical entities like caloric that could one day be eliminated.

In response, the eliminative materialist would argue that our claim to have access to our own mental states through introspection involves a distorted picture that overestimates the scope of our self-knowledge. When we introspect, we do not observe our beliefs and desires lined up on the stage of an internal theatre. Propositional attitudes are not discrete objects in our minds that we can identify and distinguish from one another like objects in the world around us. In fact, there is reason to suspect that often we do not really know what we think, believe, or desire. If this sounds implausible, think about the following example. Have you have ever had a serious argument with your partner about something you did that deeply upset him or her? When you were asked "Why did you do that?," you probably found it difficult to find an answer. You probably found yourself theorizing about your own behaviour. You might even have said things like "*Maybe* I was jealous and wanted to hurt you" or "*Maybe* I've been feeling neglected and wanted the attention." Whether or not you settle on an explanation is unimportant. What *is* important is that you aren't sure and need to *create* some kind of explanation, and so you begin positing mental states the existence of which you are not entirely sure about. What this shows is that your own mind is not really the open book you thought it was. This supports the idea that our explanations of our own behaviour are really no different from our explanations of the behaviour of others. In either case, we posit unobserved mental states in order to create a narrative that explains what we do. Introspection, then, does not necessarily give us access to a mental realm populated by mental states.

You are probably thinking that this might sound plausible for propositional attitudes but not for qualitative states of consciousness like pains. While it may be true that we often theorize about what we believe and desire, we certainly don't do this with pains. We *feel* pains; we don't posit them to explain our own behaviour. Eliminative materialists agree that we *seem to have* access to things like pains through introspection, but they deny this implies the reality of mental states. In their view all observation is **theory laden**. This means that we never make objective observations of what is before us in the world. As we perceive the world around us, we interpret what we observe, and our interpretation is shaped by what we already know or believe about the world. In other words, what we see is always coloured by our background knowledge or assumptions. This is why those who knew and accepted Ptolemy's model of the universe claimed literally to *see* the crystal spheres of the heavens turning in the night sky. In one sense, these people saw the very same thing we do when we look at the night sky, but in another very real sense what they saw was different because of the *way they saw it.* The same principles are at work in the claim that one can introspect one's own sensations. Churchland agrees that when we introspect sensations we are observing something, but he disagrees with the claim that *what* we observe are mental states. In his view, we are actually introspecting brain states. The reason it seems to us that we are observing mental states is that introspection, being a form of observation, is also theory laden. In this case, it is our acceptance of folk psychology that colours our perception. When we introspect, we expect to find mental states, and so we interpret the neural states we actually observe as though they were mental entities. Thus, although we *seem* to introspect all kinds of mental entities, and that introspection thereby appears to give us direct proof of the falsity of eliminative materialism, we have seen that this kind of argument greatly overestimates what introspection can tell us.

Why Folk Psychology Should Be Eliminated

Even if folk psychology is a theory and our mental states are theoretical entities, it does not follow from this that there are no such things as mental states, for perhaps the theory is true. In order to make plausible the claim that mental states are unreal, eliminative materialists need to provide us with reasons for thinking folk psychology should be eliminated. Once again, it is helpful to look to historical cases of successful theoretical elimination. There are two reasons theories were eliminated in the past. The first is that they suffered from predictive or explanatory inadequacies which were absent from newer, competing theories. For example, the geocentric models of the universe advocated by Aristotle and Ptolemy could not accurately predict the position of other nearby planets. The heliocentric model of Copernicus, when coupled with the new gravitational laws of Newton, did a much better job, and so there was good reason to prefer the Copernican model over Aristotle's or Ptolemy's.

The second reason theories have been eliminated is because of the desire for explanatory simplicity. If theory *B* provides a simpler explanation of a phenomenon than theory *A*, then this in itself is reason to prefer theory *B*. This reasoning involves an appeal to a principle called **Ockham's razor**: the simplest explanation of any phenomenon is probably correct. We can see this principle at work in the elimination of both caloric and the crystal spheres of the heavens. The molecular theory of heat provides a simpler explanation of the phenomena of heating and cooling than caloric theory because it does not treat heat as a substance. If we were to adopt caloric theory, we would have to say that in addition to the molecules that compose matter there is also this other stuff in the universe: caloric. A universe with caloric is a more complicated place than a universe without caloric, so if we can explain heating and cooling without caloric, we should. Similarly, a universe with concentric crystal spheres is a more complicated place than one without and requires much more complex explanations to account for the motion of other planets than a heliocentric model does. For reasons of explanatory simplicity, the heliocentric model is preferable. Thus, previous theories have been eliminated due to their predictive and explanatory inadequacies. If we can show that folk psychology suffers from similar inadequacies, then we will have reason to think it is a candidate for elimination.

Churchland's view holds that folk psychology is woefully unsuccessful as a predictive-explanatory framework. First of all, appealing to the mental states of others often fails to yield accurate predictions of behaviour. Even a simple prediction like *Don will say "Ouch" when I close the door on his finger* can turn out to be false. Perhaps Don has a high threshold for pain, or perhaps he will say nothing and punch me instead. While it is true that folk psychology helps us interact with our fellows by employing rough and ready generalizations, it is nowhere near as successful at yielding true predictions as are more reputable scientific theories. We are simply not very good at predicting what other human beings will do. Folk psychological generalizations admit far more exceptions than the laws of respectable scientific theories.

In addition to failing to provide accurate predictions, folk psychology also cannot explain many facets of human behaviour. For example, Churchland complains that it does not explain mental illness, memory, how we learn, or the nature and function of sleep, to name just a few. In fact, folk psychology fails to explain most of our cognitive abilities. Neurology and cognitive science, despite being relatively new fields of inquiry, have had considerably more success at explaining these phenomena than folk psychology, which has been around for a very long time indeed. In light of these facts, it is not unreasonable to think of folk psychology as analogous to caloric theory—a theory that could be eliminated if a more successful competing theory comes on the scene, such as a mature neuroscience, cognitive science, or something else.

Eliminative materialists point out that to claim that folk psychology will one day be eliminated does not mean that human beings will learn the language of neuroscience and stop using the language of psychology to predict and explain the behaviour of their fellows. Whatever the science that replaces folk psychology might be, we can expect it to be too complicated for the layperson to understand and employ on a daily basis. We may very well continue to use folk psychology but will do so with the realization that it is a convenient fiction or heuristic device to help us deal with other human beings effectively. Our interaction with other human beings will become much like our interaction with computers when we play chess. If you have ever played chess against a computer, you probably found that the best way to beat the computer or to remain in the game as long as possible is to try to anticipate the computer's moves. Most of us know nothing about the programming that governs the choice of moves made by the computer, so we need to rely on an alternative strategy to make our predictions. Usually what we do is pretend that the computer is another person. We treat it as though it has a collection of mental states, such as knowledge of the rules of the game, a desire to win in as few moves as possible, a desire to protect its king, and so on. This strategy generally works fairly well, but we use it with the understanding that the computer doesn't *really* have desires or other mental states. Similarly, we will continue to use folk psychology because it is practical to do so, but we will employ it with the understanding that, strictly speaking, human beings do not really have mental states.

Problems with Eliminative Materialism

The main thesis of eliminative materialism turns on the claim that folk psychology is a theory of human behaviour. If there are persuasive reasons for thinking otherwise, then eliminative materialism is in trouble. Only if folk psychology is a theory does it follow that mental states are theoretical entities that are subject to potential elimination. Thus, an effective way to attack eliminative materialism is to show that there are reasons for thinking folk psychology is not a theory. One of the arguments Churchland offered to convince us of the theoretical status of folk psychology was the claim that folk psychological explanations follow the same pattern as scientific explanations. That is, they are DN explanations. There is some reason to doubt this is true.

Suppose we want to explain why Janis took her umbrella with her to work. Identifying her mental states seems to do the job admirably. For instance, if we say that she *believed* it was going to rain and that she had a *desire* to keep dry, these claims about her appear to satisfy our need for an explanation. How exactly does the identification of Janis's mental states explain her behaviour? Churchland would have us believe that we implicitly appealed to a set of folk psychological generalizations and that from these, coupled with a description of the initial conditions, we deduced Janis's action. Among these generalizations we might include claims like *people who believe it is going to rain tend to take precautions that will enable them to keep dry*, and *if people believe doing x will help them keep dry, and they want to keep dry, they will tend to do x*. While it is probably the case that one could employ these generalizations to construct a deductive argument with

Janis's action as the conclusion, this is not the only way that referring to Janis's mental states can explain her behaviour.

To see this we need to appreciate that generalizations like the ones above are *normative*. That is, they describe the way people *ought* to behave if they are *rational beings*. These are unlike the laws of nature employed in DN explanations. Laws of nature describe the way things *must* behave, not how they *should* behave. Rationality, then, plays a very important role in our folk psychological explanations. In fact, one might argue that it plays the central role. It is an interesting feature of Janis's action that it is the sort of thing a rational person would ordinarily do. That is, when we explain her behaviour by appealing to what Janis believed and desired, her taking her umbrella to work seems like the rational thing to do, and, furthermore, such an action is predictable only on the assumption that Janis generally behaves in a rational manner. That is, given that Janis believed it was going to rain, and given that she had a desire to stay dry, it was rational for her to carry her umbrella to work.

In light of this, it is tempting to provide an alternative account of how folk psychological explanations function. The reason the identification of someone's mental states explains their behaviour is that doing so places the behaviour in a context that reveals the rationality of the agent. Since human beings are rational animals, to render behaviour rational *is* to explain it. This is why we feel so strongly that thoroughly irrational behaviour is inexplicable or else needs to be explained by appealing to something other than mental states, such as a neural anomaly. That is, because we can't render the behaviour rational by identifying the agent's mental states, we need to rely on other kinds of explanations, but then we are not using folk psychology.

If the competing account of psychological explanation is correct, then there is reason to be sceptical of the claim that folk psychology is a theory. The argument for the claim that folk psychology is a theory depended on there being similarities between folk psychology and theories generally. Thus, each difference we discover in the workings of folk psychology and the workings of other theories, such as the way they explain phenomena, counts against the idea that folk psychology is a theory. If folk psychology is not a theory, then it cannot be a candidate for theoretical elimination in the future.

A second problem with the argument for eliminative materialism concerns the claim that folk psychology is a bad theory because it does a relatively poor job of predicting and explaining human behaviour. If folk psychology isn't a theory in the first place, as the first objection suggests, then we ought not to be overly concerned about the fact that it does not give us terribly accurate predictions of behaviour. If the generalizations of folk psychology are normative rather than nomological, then *of course* we can't always predict how people will act on the basis of what we know about their psychology. People don't always act rationally. Since folk psychology isn't a theory, we shouldn't expect it to provide accurate predictions in the first place. If a scientific theory yields even one false prediction, this is usually reason enough to think it is a bad theory and ought to be abandoned or amended. By contrast, if the generalizations we appeal to in order to make predictions are not part of a theory, that is no reason to abandon the generalizations so long as they work most of the time and so long as we refuse to treat them as laws.

Similar considerations can be brought to bear on the other explanatory failures Churchland attributes to folk psychology.

We can admit that our commonsense psychological framework does not explain phenomena like sleep, learning, or mental illness, but we should wonder *why* folk psychology ought to explain these things. Even if folk psychology were a theory, it is unclear why these kinds of phenomena ought to fall within its purview. Coughing, like learning and the other phenomena Churchland mentions, is a form of human behaviour, but we don't expect to be able to explain why people cough by talking about their mental states. Instead, we look for a physiological explanation. Why should learning or mental illness be any different? It is hardly surprising that such things will be more adequately explained by neurology or cognitive science. One can hardly fault folk psychology for failing to do something it is not supposed to do. In order to show that folk psychology really does suffer from a host of explanatory failures, one needs to show it is the business of folk psychology to explain these things in the first place, and it is difficult to see why anyone would think it is.

Suppose that Churchland and other eliminative materialists were able to muster additional arguments to convince us that folk psychology really is a theory, that it offers inadequate explanations and predictions of behaviour, and that neuroscience can explain these phenomena much better. Would it follow that there are no such things as mental states? Not necessarily. It is interesting to note that in the case of historically successful theoretical eliminations, we have not seen a wholesale rejection of the ontology of the eliminated theories. When scientists abandoned caloric theory, they concluded that there is no such thing as caloric, but caloric theory did not include caloric alone. It also involved concepts such as heat, temperature, and physical objects. While no one today believes caloric exists, most of us continue to believe in heat, temperature, and physical objects. Thus, when caloric theory was eliminated, some of the concepts used by that theory remained behind. Similarly, when astronomers abandoned the Ptolemaic model of the universe, they concluded that there is no such thing as the crystal spheres, but Ptolemy's theory consisted of more than these. It also involved the planets, the sun, and the stars—things we continue to believe in today. Thus, even when a theory is eliminated and replaced by a better one, we do not usually see the elimination of *all* the entities to which the earlier theory appealed. Sometimes many of them are incorporated into the new theory. The moral here for the future of folk psychology should be clear. Even if it is eliminated and replaced by another theory, it doesn't follow that the new theory will not include mental states in its ontology.

Eliminative materialism has gained considerable notoriety, but despite this it has few adherents, largely because most philosophers are not convinced by the arguments presented in favour of the idea that folk psychology is a theory. Most philosophers think there are such things as mental states but prefer to identify them with physical phenomena.

Suggestions for Further Reading

Churchland, P. 1970. "The Logical Character of Action Explanations." *Philosophical Review* 79: 214–36.

Churchland, P. 1981. "Eliminative Materialism and Propositional Attitudes." *Journal of Philosophy* 78: 67–90.

Churchland, P. 1985. "Reduction, Qualia, and the Direct Introspection of Brain States." *Journal of Philosophy* 82: 8–28.

Greenwood, J.D. 1991. *The Future of Folk Psychology: Intentionality and Cognitive Science.* Cambridge; New York: Cambridge University Press.

Rorty, R. 1970. "In Defence of Eliminative Materialism." *Review of Metaphysics* 24: 112–21.

CHAPTER 7

■ SUPERVENIENCE

What is Supervenience?

When Donald Davidson advanced anomalous monism as a form of physicalism, he supplemented it with an alternative way of describing the relationship he thought exists between the mental and the physical: he claimed that the mental *supervenes* on the physical. Although anomalous monism itself was not widely adopted by philosophers, many endorsed **supervenience** as a promising account of the mind-body relation. After Davidson introduced supervenience to philosophers of mind, Jaegwon Kim did a great deal to popularize and explore the nuances of this concept.

Supervenience itself is kind of *relation*. It describes the way certain sorts of things are related to one another, or how they are connected. Relations are often of philosophical interest because some important concepts are *fundamentally* relational. The concept of a *parent* is a good example. This concept must be understood in terms of the *relationship* between a mother or father and their child. The items related by supervenience are usually **families of properties**, the traits or characteristics possessed by objects or events. For instance, an object such as a ball has certain properties, including being round, red, a certain size, a certain texture, etc., and the event of my stubbing my toe has certain properties, such as being quick, painful, distracting, and so on. A *family* of properties is simply a group of properties of the same kind or type. A family of properties can be as large or small a group as we like, depending on the kinds of properties we are interested in. For instance, *colour properties* is a family of properties that includes the property of being orange, the property of being red, the property of being blue, and so on.

When two families of properties are related by supervenience, we say that one set or family of properties *supervenes* on the other family of properties. The supervening properties are called **supervenient properties** and the properties on which these supervene are variously described as the **supervenience base**, the **subvenient properties**, or often just the **base properties**.

Philosophers who are attracted to supervenience tend to think of the world as being layered. This is similar to the view of the world adopted by the advocates of the unity of science described in Chapter 3. At the core of this way of thinking about the world is the idea that what happens at more basic levels determines what happens at higher levels. For instance, we believe that the behaviour of cells depends on the behaviour of the molecules that make them up, or that large-scale phenomena such as national economies depend on the spending habits of individuals. What distinguishes supervenience from the unity of science is that supervenience denies that higher-level facts can be reduced to the lower-level facts on which they depend.

There can be many kinds of supervenience depending upon which families of properties it relates. As a philosophical concept, supervenience was first employed in aesthetics and moral philosophy. Before we explore its use in the philosophy of mind, it would be useful to examine these earlier versions to help clarify the general concept further.

Supervenience in Aesthetics and Moral Philosophy

Aesthetics is the philosophical study of beauty. Philosophers in this field employed supervenience to describe the relationship between aesthetic and non-aesthetic properties. Aesthetic properties are **evaluative** properties, such as being beautiful, ugly, graceful, or clumsy. Non-aesthetic properties are **descriptive** properties that are non-evaluative. To appreciate the difference, let's consider an example. If you look at a painting and say that it is red and yellow, you simply describe it and thereby identify its descriptive properties. By contrast, if you say of the same painting that it is beautiful, you are no longer *describing* it, you are *evaluating* it as a good painting. Thus, we would say that the redness and yellowness of the painting are non-aesthetic properties, whereas its beauty is an aesthetic property.

Aesthetic properties are quite different from descriptive properties in an interesting way. The descriptive properties of a painting are easy to distinguish from one another and to identify. One can write a list of all the colours on the canvass, divide the painting into a grid and plot the location of different coloured brush strokes, and even identify the chemical composition that makes up the pigment of each colour on the canvass. The beauty of the painting, however, is much more elusive. Beauty is not something we can isolate and map in the way we can with redness. One cannot point to a certain part of the painting and say "There's the beauty" in the way one can point to a part of the painting and say "There's the colour red." Furthermore, while we do not ordinarily disagree about the colour of some part of a painting, we often disagree about whether or not a painting is beautiful. Although aesthetic properties are clearly quite different from non-aesthetic properties, it is clear that what makes a painting beautiful or ugly is the collection and organization of its non-aesthetic properties. Although the colours and brush strokes on the canvass are not themselves beautiful, the way in which they are combined with one another (and all the other descriptive elements of the painting) makes a painting beautiful. Hence, the aesthetic properties of a work of art *depend on*, and are *determined by*, its non-aesthetic properties.

The way in which the beauty of a work of art depends on its non-aesthetic properties is a very complex matter. Although it is clear that aesthetic properties depend on non-aesthetic properties, it seems very implausible to suggest that aesthetic properties could be reduced to non-aesthetic properties. There are at least two reasons for this.

In classical versions of reductionism, the bridge laws connecting two theories not only were supposed to allow us to *reduce* the phenomena of one theory to the phenomena of a more fundamental theory, but also to *deduce* or predict higher-level phenomena from lower-level phenomena. For example, the bridge laws connecting cellular biology and chemistry were supposed to allow us to predict cellular phenomena from knowledge of chemical phenomena. One reason for being sceptical of the idea of reducing aesthetic to non-aesthetic properties is that there don't appear to be laws connecting aesthetic and non-aesthetic properties that would enable us to deduce the aesthetic properties of a work of art from knowledge of its non-aesthetic properties. Our aesthetic experiences are simply not like this. We do not observe the non-aesthetic properties of a painting and then, using a set of rules, conclude that the painting is beautiful. The fact that a painting is beautiful is not something that we work out or calculate on the basis of other facts. If there were rules about which non-aesthetic properties give rise to aesthetic properties, presumably there wouldn't be so many terrible paintings in the world, for creating a good painting would simply be a matter of following the appropriate rules.

The second reason we should be sceptical about the idea that one can reduce aesthetic to non-aesthetic properties is similar to the reason for being sceptical about reducing mental types to physical types. Just as the same kind of mental state can exist in creatures that are physically different, the same aesthetic property can be supported by radically different non-aesthetic properties. For example, paintings, sculptures, and symphonies have radically different non-aesthetic properties and yet can share the same aesthetic properties since they can all be beautiful. In light of this fact, one might say that aesthetic properties are *multiply realizable*, for they can be realized by a wide array of non-aesthetic properties. As we have already seen, multiple realizability is a serious obstacle to reduction. The fact that aesthetic properties also seem to be multiply realizable appears to raise the same obstacle to attempts to reduce aesthetic to non-aesthetic properties.

It seems that aesthetic properties depend on non-aesthetic properties but cannot be reduced to them. Philosophers introduced the term *supervenience* to describe this relationship and to contrast it with reduction. Thus, the proposal was that aesthetic properties like beauty *supervene* on non-aesthetic properties like colour, shape, and so on. Aesthetic properties are therefore *supervenient* properties while descriptive or non-aesthetic properties are the *base properties* on which the supervenient properties depend. As a relation, however, supervenience was meant to express more than a form of dependence without reduction; it was also intended to capture a form of consistency in the relationship between aesthetic and non-aesthetic properties. The idea is that since the aesthetic properties of a work of art depend on its non-aesthetic properties, any two works of art with the same descriptive properties must have the same aesthetic value. Thus, if two paintings are indistinguishable, they *must* be equally beautiful or ugly; it is impossible for them to differ in their aesthetic properties if they have the same descriptive properties. Supervenience in aesthetics, then, is a concept designed to capture three ideas about the relationship between aesthetic and non-aesthetic properties:

1. Aesthetic properties *depend* on non-aesthetic properties.
2. Aesthetic properties *cannot be reduced* to non-aesthetic properties.

3. The relation between aesthetic and non-aesthetic properties holds *consistently* across individual works of art.

To say that aesthetic properties supervene on non-aesthetic properties is therefore just a shorthand way of expressing these three ideas.

To further enhance our understanding of supervenience, let's consider its use in ethics and draw out the parallels with its use in aesthetics. Ethics is the philosophical study of morally right and wrong behaviour. Here the proposal was that supervenience might be a useful way to understand the relationship between moral and non-moral properties. A **moral property** is, like beauty in aesthetics, an evaluative property such as the property of being good, honourable, or evil. **Non-moral properties** are similar to the non-aesthetic properties we discussed earlier; they are not evaluative but are *descriptive*. When we talk about a person, we can either describe that person and all the actions they perform in non-moral terms, or we can evaluate that person morally. For instance, to say that *Jones held the door open so Frank could enter without putting down his parcels* simply describes what Jones did. To say that *Jones was chivalrous* evaluates Jones morally; it is to say that he is a good man.

In one important sense, Jones's goodness is a quite different kind of thing from his behaviour and other descriptive properties. Jones's behaviour consists of all the actions he has ever performed. We could create a long list of these in completely value-neutral terms. That is, we could simply describe everything Jones does without saying anything about whether what he does is good or bad. If we wanted to, we could simply describe each action in terms of how Jones's body moved around in the world in relation to other bodies and objects. These descriptions would include only non-moral properties. All of the properties that would be involved in such descriptions are empirically observable; that is, we can agree on whether or not Jones has these descriptive properties simply by watching him. Jones's goodness, however, seems to be a different matter. Being good is not like holding the door open with the right arm: it is not something that we see or locate among the descriptive properties of an action. This is true even for more extreme actions like killing. Among Jones's descriptive properties might be the property of stabbing Smith. We can all see what Jones did (i.e., that he stabbed Smith) but the goodness or badness of Jones (i.e., his moral property) is not empirically identifiable.

Despite the fact that moral properties are not empirically observable, most philosophers believe they *depend* on non-moral properties. That is, although goodness or badness is not a property we can identify alongside the descriptive properties that make up a person's actions, it nevertheless seems clear that a person's moral properties depend on the actions they perform. We might say that Jones is bad *in virtue* of the fact that he stabbed Smith, even though Jones's badness is not a property we can observe in him when he performs that action. The form this dependence takes is very much like the kind of dependence we saw in aesthetics. There is good reason to think that although moral properties depend on non-moral properties, the former cannot be reduced to the latter.

The main reason for this is that, like beauty, goodness also seems to be multiply realizable. We can easily imagine that Ann and Sally are both good people even though they have performed different actions. Even if they do some of the same things, it is easy to suppose that they don't perform them in exactly the same way. Thus, although Ann and Sally have completely different non-moral properties, it is still possible for them to have the same moral properties (i.e., they can both be good). This possibility creates a serious obstacle to reducing moral properties to non-moral properties, for the possibility of reduction seems to require that only the same kinds of actions can be good.

The possibility of two individuals with the same moral properties but different non-moral properties appears to preclude the possibility of reducing the former to the latter, but what shall we say of two people who have all the same descriptive properties? If Ann and Sally had all the same descriptive properties in common (i.e., they do all the same things in the same way), then in light of the claim that moral properties depend on non-moral properties, we would have to say that Ann and Sally are either both good or both bad. It would be *impossible* for one of them to be good and for the other to be bad. Thus, just as two identical paintings cannot differ with respect to their aesthetic properties, two people performing the same actions cannot differ with respect to their moral properties.

To capture all of these ideas about how moral properties are related to non-moral properties, philosophers have proposed that moral properties *supervene* on non-moral properties. In this case, the moral properties make up the supervenient family and the non-moral properties constitute the supervenience base. Thus, in ethics we see the concept of supervenience was used to capture three ideas that are exactly analogous to the ones in aesthetics:

1. Moral properties *depend* on non-moral properties.
2. Moral properties *cannot be reduced* to non-moral properties.
3. The relation between moral and non-moral properties holds *consistently* across individual moral agents.

If we abstract from our specific examples of supervenience relations in aesthetics and ethics, we see that as a general kind of relation, supervenience describes a relationship between two families of properties of the following kind:

1. Supervenient properties *depend* on base properties.
2. Supervenient properties *cannot be reduced* to base properties.
3. The relation between supervenient and base properties holds *consistently* across individuals.

Now that we have a clearer idea of what supervenience is all about, let's examine its use in the philosophy of mind.

Psychophysical Supervenience

Philosophers of mind developed an interest in supervenience because it seemed to be a promising way to describe the relationship between the mental and the physical, since it seemed to satisfy two needs philosophers thought were required for a plausible theory of mind. The first need was for a non-reductive theory. Because supervenience denies that supervenient properties can be reduced to base properties, it seemed to fit the bill admirably. The second need was to express a form of physicalism despite the denial of reduction. Some philosophers began to think that the best way to achieve this was not by denying the existence of non-physical states, but by claiming that the mental *depends* on the physical. This falls short of the more robust forms of physicalism such as eliminative materialism or the identity theory, but remains a form of materialism because it claims that the physical facts in the world determine *all* the facts, including *all the mental facts*. Since supervenience expresses a form of dependence as well as anti-reductionism, supervenience looked very appealing indeed.

Since supervenience describes a relationship between families of properties, adopting this relation for use in the philosophy of mind meant changing the focus from talk about mental *states* or *events* to talk about mental *properties*, such as the property of being a belief, or the property of being painful. The proposal, then, was that mental properties supervene on physical properties. This is known as **psychophysical supervenience.**

Once philosophers began to explore the possibility of using supervenience to express a form of non-reductive physicalism, it became apparent that there are several different ways in which one can formulate or express it. There are two distinguishing features of the relation that, depending on how they are understood, create different versions of psychophysical supervenience.

Strong and Weak Psychophysical Supervenience

We saw earlier that one of the ideas supervenience was

supposed to capture is the requirement that supervenient properties depend on base properties in a manner that is *consistent*. In aesthetics this amounted to the claim that if two paintings have all the same non-aesthetic properties, they *must* have the same aesthetic properties; in ethics this was expressed by the claim that if two people have all the same non-moral properties, they *must* have the same moral properties. Philosophers of mind also thought that this kind of consistency was important. In the case of psychophysical supervenience they proposed that if two individuals or two worlds have all the same physical properties, then they *must* have the same mental properties.

The word "must" appears in each of these formulations of the consistency requirement. Depending on how we understand this word, we can have two versions of supervenience. On one reading of the word "must" all that is intended in the claim that *Individuals with the same physical properties must have the same mental properties* is the idea that it *just so happens* that physical indiscernibility is *always* accompanied by mental indiscernibility, but that it doesn't have to be that way. In this case, the relationship between mental and physical properties is **contingent**. The other, stronger reading of "must" claims that physical indiscernibility *has to* be accompanied by mental indiscernibility. In this case, the relationship between mental and physical properties is not contingent, but is **necessary**.

Philosophers often express this distinction in terms of claims about possible worlds. **Possible worlds** are imaginary universes that are just like the actual one, except for certain specifiable differences. For instance, if you have ever imagined what your life would have been like if you never went to university, you were imagining another possible world. In this other possible world, everything is the same as it is in the actual world, except for the fact that you didn't go to university, plus everything that depended on that decision. If a claim is necessary, then it is true in *all* possible worlds. By contrast, if a claim is contingent, it is true in *some* possible worlds, but not in others. Let's use a couple of examples to help illustrate these ideas.

As a matter of fact, all chlorophyll is green. Since we never have chlorophyll in the actual world that isn't green, we can say that chlorophyll *must* be green. However, we can certainly imagine another possible world in which chlorophyll is red (perhaps because our sun emits different wavelengths of electromagnetic radiation in this other possible world). Thus, when we say that chlorophyll *must* be green, we are making a contingent claim. We are saying that it just happens to be the case that all chlorophyll is green, but that things don't have to be that way. If our sun were different, chlorophyll might have been red.

Now contrast the claim that chlorophyll must be green with the claim that triangles must be three-sided. Can you imagine another possible world in which triangles are not three-sided? You can probably imagine another possible world in which we use the word "square" to refer to three-sided figures, but this does not mean triangles aren't three-sided in that world. The *concept* of a triangle is unaffected by the word we use to refer to that concept. Triangles are what they are (three-sided figures) *regardless* of what we call them. So instead of thinking about referring to triangles using words like "square," try imagining a triangle that has five sides instead of three. Were you successful? I'll bet you weren't. When you imagine a five-sided triangle, you are imagining a pentagram rather than a triangle. It is impossible to imagine a triangle that doesn't have three sides. So, it is possible to imagine other possible worlds in which chlorophyll is not green, but it is *not* possible to imagine other possible worlds in which triangles are not three-sided. The point of this comparison is to show that when we say that triangles *must* have three sides we are making a stronger claim than when we say that chlorophyll *must* be green. The former claim is true in *all* possible worlds, whereas the latter claim, which is merely contingent, is true only of *some* possible worlds.

If we describe the relationship between mental and physical properties as a contingent relation, this gives us **weak supervenience.** According to weak supervenience, when we say that two people with the same physical properties *must* have the same mental properties, all we are saying is that it just *happens to be the case* that any two people with the same physical properties will have the same mental properties. For example, if Tanya had a physical twin in this world (i.e., someone with all the same physical properties as Tanya, not to be confused with a birth-twin), they would both have the same mental states. However, if Tanya had a twin in some other possible world, *that* twin could have entirely different mental properties or perhaps no mental properties at all. Perhaps Tanya's twin is a zombie in every possible world but this one.

By contrast, if we characterize the relationship between mental and physical properties as necessary, this gives us **strong supervenience.** According to strong supervenience, it is *impossible* for two people with the same physical properties to have different mental properties. Thus, if mental properties strongly supervene on physical properties, then, provided that Tanya and her twin are physically identical in every world, they will have the same mental properties in every possible world.

There is much disagreement about which form of psychophysical supervenience best captures the relationship between mind and body. Most of these disputes are far too technical for us to investigate here; however, there is one issue we should focus on in light of its significance for regarding supervenience as a form of physicalism. Some philosophers have argued that neither weak nor strong supervenience actually expresses the *dependence* of mental properties on physical properties. If this is true, then supervenience cannot be used to express a form of physicalism as philosophers intended it to do. If we admit that mental properties do not depend on physical properties, we have surrendered the minimum condition that is required for physicalism, for in this case the physical no longer determines all the mental facts about the world.

Psychophysical Supervenience and Psychophysical Dependence

Although Jaegwon Kim did more than most philosophers to explore, refine, and popularize supervenience as a philosophical concept, in the end he became one of its most influential critics. He has levelled several extremely powerful arguments designed to undermine the claim that psychophysical supervenience expresses the dependence of the mental on the physical. If his arguments are successful, then supervenience cannot represent a form of physicalism, for a minimal condition of physicalism is that mental properties depend on, and are determined by, physical properties.

According to weak supervenience, mental properties supervene on physical properties in this world, but there is nothing necessary about this. As we saw, according to weak supervenience, there are other possible worlds in which you may have physical duplicates that lack mental properties altogether; they have the same degree of consciousness as rocks do in this world. What we see with weak supervenience, then, is that the connection between mental properties and physical properties is so weak that mental properties can vary without any corresponding variation in physical properties. In Kim's view, this possibility renders the relationship between mental and physical properties too weak to capture any genuine relation of dependence. His reasoning is as follows: if your mental properties really did depend on your physical properties, then it shouldn't be possible in any world for your physical duplicates to have mental properties that are different from yours. Since mental properties *can* vary without any corresponding variation in physical properties (e.g., your physical duplicates in other possible worlds are zombies), it would seem that mental properties do not actually depend on physical properties.

To clarify this further, let's consider an analogy with supervenience in aesthetics. If aesthetic properties supervene *weakly* on non-aesthetic properties, this allows for the following possibility: there are identical paintings in two different possible worlds. In one world the painting is beautiful, and in the other world it is ugly. If the (descriptively) same painting can be both ugly and beautiful, then it seems that its aesthetic properties cannot be determined by its descriptive or non-aesthetic properties. Here's why. How do we explain why one painting is beautiful and the other (identical) painting is ugly? Since the paintings are descriptively identical, we can't explain the aesthetic difference by appealing to non-aesthetic differences, such as the colours or brush strokes on the canvass. The only other option is that there must be *some third factor* aside from the non-aesthetic properties of the painting that explains this difference in evaluative properties. (Perhaps in the other possible world there is a convention that a work of art is beautiful only if it was painted before the twentieth century.) If a third factor is required to explain why one painting is beautiful and the other is ugly, the aesthetic properties of the paintings must be determined by that third factor. But if this is so, the aesthetic properties of the paintings do not depend on their non-aesthetic properties; they depend on the third factor (aesthetic conventions of some sort). Weak supervenience expresses a relationship between aesthetic and non-aesthetic properties, but we now have reason to believe the former do not depend on the latter. In this case, weak supervenience doesn't express a form of dependence after all.

Keeping this argument from aesthetics in mind, let's see how the same kind of considerations undermine the idea that weak psychophysical supervenience expresses a form of dependence. If you and your twin are physically identical and yet mentally different, something else (i.e., some third factor) must account for those mental differences (since by hypothesis there aren't any physical differences). If something other than your physical properties determines why you have mental properties and your twin does not, it can't be true that your mental properties depend on your physical properties; instead, they must depend on the unidentified third factor. (It is hard to imagine what that might be, though looking back to parallelism we might say that God could be such a third factor.) Since weak psychophysical supervenience expresses a relationship between your mental and physical properties and your mental properties depend on something other than your physical properties (God's will, for instance), weak psychophysical supervenience does not express a form of dependence.

According to strong supervenience, your physical duplicate in every possible world is *also* your mental duplicate. There cannot be mental differences between you and your physical duplicates *without* corresponding physical differences. (This is consistent with multiple realization because strong supervenience claims only that physical indiscernibility entails mental indiscernibility, not that two mentally identical beings must be physically identical.) Because strong supervenience employs a stronger form of necessity than weak supervenience, one might think that it does not fall prey to the same objection as weak supervenience. However, Kim argues that it succumbs to similar problems.

Here's the difficulty. Strong supervenience tells us only that there is a relationship between mental properties and physical properties, such that any two individuals with the same physical properties will have the same mental properties in all possible worlds. Thus, if there is some *mental* variation or difference between you and your twin in some other possible world, there must be a corresponding *physical* difference between you. To say this is simply to say that mental and physical properties *co-vary*: changes in one family of properties are always accompanied by changes in the other family of properties. The difficulty with this is that mere **covariance** between two families of properties does not necessarily imply that one family of properties depends on the other. This is because there are three possible ways of explaining why these properties co-vary.

The first reason mental and physical properties co-vary could be that mental properties depend on physical properties, as physicalists maintain. That is, if mental properties actually depend on physical properties, that would explain why changes in the one are always accompanied by changes in the other. If mental properties depend on physical properties, they would have to change along with changes in the physical properties on which they depend.

The second explanation is that physical properties depend on mental properties. Again, if physical properties depend on mental properties this also explains why changes in mental properties are always accompanied by changes in physical properties. This, of course, is precisely the opposite of what physicalists want because it gives the mental priority over the physical. Physicalists want mental facts to *be determined* by physical facts, not *to determine* physical facts. If this is the reason mental properties supervene on physical properties, supervenience certainly can't be regarded as a form of physicalism and so falls far short of capturing the ideas it was supposed to.

The third reason mental and physical properties co-vary could be that both properties depend on an unidentified third property. Kim uses intelligence and manual dexterity to illustrate this possibility. Imagine that intelligence and manual dexterity co-vary in every possible world. Is it really plausible to say that intelligence depends on manual dexterity, or that manual dexterity depends on intelligence? It seems not. What is more plausible is that both of these properties depend on a third property, likely some genetic property. Since manual dexterity and intelligence both depend on a common genetic property, they will co-vary with one another. If your twin in some other possible world is more intelligent than you, then he or she is different from you at the genetic level, but if this is so, then your twin will also be more manually dexterous because dexterity depends on the same genetic factors. Thus, we see differences in intelligence varying along with differences in manual dexterity, but not because one depends on the other. The lesson here for strong psychophysical supervenience is that the covariance between mental and physical properties might be due to an unidentified third family of properties, in which case the fact that mental properties strongly supervene on physical properties is no guarantee that mental properties depend on physical properties.

The challenge for philosophers is that strong supervenience itself does not tell us which of these three possible explanations is correct. Each one is consistent with strong psychophysical supervenience, and yet only one of these possibilities constitutes a form of physicalism. Because of the way supervenience has been understood and formulated, it clearly falls well short of the goals philosophers originally had for it. Supervenience was supposed to express a special kind of dependence of the mental on the physical, but once the relation was given a specific form (weak or strong supervenience) it fell well short of philosophers' expectations. Supervenience tells us only that mental properties co-vary with physical properties; it does not explain why the covariance happens. To explain that would be to solve the mind-body problem. This is why many critics of supervenience claim that it is not, despite initial hopes to the contrary, a solution to the mind-body problem, but is rather an expression of the problem itself.

Suggestions for Further Reading

Campbell, N. 2000. "Supervenience and Psycho-Physical Dependence." *Dialogue: Canadian Philosophical Review* 39: 303-16.

Davidson, D. 1970. "Mental Events." *Experience and Theory*. Ed. L. Foster and J. Swanson. Amherst, MA: University of Massachusetts Press.

Hare, R.M. 1952. *The Language of Morals*. Oxford: Clarendon Press.

Kim, J. 1982. "Psychophysical Supervenience." *Philosophical Studies* 41: 51-70.

Kim, J. 1990. "Supervenience as a Philosophical Concept." *Metaphilosophy* 21: 1-27.

CHAPTER 8

■ MENTAL CONTENT

What is Mental Content?

I n the introduction to this book we saw that mental states
fall into two categories: propositional attitudes and qualitative states of consciousness. Propositional attitudes include
mental states such as beliefs, desires, fears, doubts, and so on;
they are states that involve an attitude (*believing, desiring*, etc.)
toward an actual or possible state of affairs (for example, that
Greece will win the European Cup). Thus, one may be said to
believe, desire, fear, or doubt that Greece will win the European
Cup. Qualitative states of consciousness, on the other hand,
are the intrinsic, "felt" qualities of experience, such as the
painfulness of pain, the redness of the sensation of red, and so
on. While there are important differences between these two
kinds of mental states, we noted that they share one essential
feature: intentionality. This is the relation of *aboutness* that
Franz Brentano claimed is common to *all* mental states and is

what, in his view, distinguishes the mental from the non-mental. Even false beliefs and visual hallucinations have this feature. For example, if Shanna believes that unicorns exist, her belief is *about* the non-actual state of affairs that unicorns exist. Similarly, if Bob has taken a narcotic and hallucinates that I am wearing red lipstick, he is aware *of* the redness of the imagined lipstick.

What our mental states are about is more naturally described as **mental content**. That is, we can say that the *content* of Shanna's belief is that unicorns exist and that the *content* of Bob's experience is the redness of my imagined lipstick. Thus, mental content is *what* we believe, desire, fear, or experience. What has struck many philosophers about Brentano's thesis is that the intentionality of mental states implies that they are **representational**. Just as a photograph represents the scene it captures, mental states represent the way the world is or could be. We can express the content of Shanna's belief in terms of the notion of representation by saying that, through her beliefs, Shanna *represents* the world as one that contains unicorns. Similarly, to say that Bob is aware of the redness of my imagined lipstick is to say that Bob's visual experience *represents* my lips as being a certain colour.

Before we begin to explore a central puzzle about mental content it is important to recognize that Brentano's claim that all mental states have intentionality or representational content is a controversial one. While it seems clear that most mental states have representational content, it is far from obvious that all of them do. Consider pain, for example. When I feel pain I do not appear to be representing a real or imagined object (such as Bob's imagined lipstick) in a certain way. The painfulness of the pain does not seem to be about anything; it simply exists. The same could be said about moods. Moods are clearly mental states that have a qualitative dimension. It feels a certain way to be happy or depressed, yet it is difficult to associate any particular representational content with such states. Of course, it is possible to be depressed about some particular state of affairs. For instance, I can be depressed about the death of a loved one, in which case my mental state has a quite specific representational content: I am representing the death of a loved one as sad, unfortunate, or depressing. This is not significantly different from representing lipstick as red or representing the world as one that contains unicorns. This kind of depression, however, is not what I had in mind when I introduced the idea of a mood. By "mood" I mean a *general state of mind* or *outlook* which is quite different from being depressed or happy about something *in particular.* To feel depressed in general (what is sometimes called "objectless depression") is not directed at any *particular* state of affairs. What could we say is represented by this kind of depression? The answer is unclear.

Those who think that all mental content is representational have attempted to respond to these concerns. They claim that although pains and moods seem to be different from other mental states, they have representational content nevertheless. In the case of pain they propose that this sensation represents the part of the body where the pain is felt and represents it as *painful* in order to indicate real or imagined bodily damage. When it comes to moods like depression, it has been suggested that the individual in question represents *everything* as being worthless, pointless, or uninteresting. The depression, then, works like a filter that alters the way the world *in general* is experienced or represented.

It is unclear how to evaluate such proposals and philosophers continue to be divided on this question. Some claim, with Brentano, that all mental states have representational content. Others admit that while some experiential states are representational, many of them are not. Still others maintain that only propositional attitudes have representational content. Regardless of which of these views is correct, it is clear that many mental states have content. The task philosophers face, then, is to understand what makes a mental state have the content it does.

Internalism and Externalism

Arguably, the most significant debate about mental content is the one between internalists and externalists. The point of disagreement here is about how we should **individuate** mental states. Individuating mental states is a matter of distinguishing mental states that are the same from those that are different, such as the belief that the sky is blue from the belief that grass is green. Obviously, the content of mental states plays a central role here. We usually distinguish between the belief that the sky is blue and the belief that grass is green by pointing out that the content of these states is different since one is about the sky and the other is about grass. However, this is helpful only if we *already* know what makes a mental state have the content it does, and this is a controversial matter. Suppose that John and Heather both believe that *water is thirst quench-ing*. It probably seems obvious that they are thinking the same thought (i.e., that their mental states have the same content), but depending on the factors that determine the content of their respective beliefs, John and Heather might actually be thinking about quite different things. Thus, agreeing on the factors that determine mental content is crucial if we are to use mental content as a means of individuating mental states.

Internalists and externalists have quite different approaches to this issue. **Internalists** claim that the content of a mental state is primarily a matter of features intrinsic to the person who has it. **Externalists**, on the other hand, think that what a mental state is about is primarily a relational matter. To appre-ciate what distinguishes internalists from externalists we need a better understanding of the difference between intrinsic and relational properties. Although this distinction is itself some-what controversial, the main idea can be expressed as follows. **Intrinsic properties** are characteristics that things have in isolation from other things. The size of your brain, the fact it is composed primarily of nervous tissue, and whether or not you have an appendix are all examples of intrinsic properties; these are properties you have regardless of your surroundings or rela-tionships to other things or people. Granted, you wouldn't exist if your parents didn't exist and so couldn't have a brain or appendix if they hadn't brought you into the world, but your existence (and your having a brain and appendix) does not continue to depend on your parents. If they ceased to exist, you, your brain, and your appendix would not suddenly disappear.

Relational properties, by contrast, are entirely a matter of *relationships* between things. Two examples of relational properties are *being next to* and *being an aunt*. The property of being next to the coffee table is nothing more than the relationship between an object and the coffee table. If I move a book from the chair next to the coffee table and place it on top of the coffee table, nothing about the book itself changes—it still has the same number of pages, the same cover, and the same text—but its relation to the coffee table is altered. Similarly, when someone becomes an aunt she does not undergo any physical change; in fact, one can become an aunt without ever knowing it. There is no physical test one can perform on an individual to determine whether or not she is an aunt. The only change that occurs is relational: becoming an aunt is simply a matter of standing in a new relationship to another person.

Now that we are clear about the notion of intrinsic and relational properties, we can say a little more about internalism and externalism. When internalists claim that mental content is a matter of the intrinsic properties of a thinker, they mean that the content is determined by physical processes *inside* the thinker's body, such as their brain states. Externalists, by contrast, claim that the content of a mental state is primarily a matter of relationships to things *outside* the thinker, such as their linguistic community, their causal or evolutionary history, or even their physical environment. Thus, the debate between internalists and externalists is often put in terms of the question, "Is mental content a matter of what is going on in one's head?" Internalists claim it is, and externalists deny this.

This does not mean that internalists think that what happens outside one's head is insignificant. Suppose I am looking at a lemon under normal conditions and come to believe that I am looking at a lemon. How do I come to have this belief? While a complete answer is currently beyond our grasp, we have some idea of what is involved. Light waves reflect off the surface of the lemon and strike my retinas, which send signals through the optic nerve to my brain, which generates a series of complex brain processes that are identical with or in some way underlie my belief that I am looking at a lemon. Obviously, factors outside my head are very important to my coming to have the belief that I do. What the internalist would point out, however, is that the *very same belief* could have been caused in some other way. It is not difficult to imagine a scenario in which I have all the same experiences and thoughts I do now, but exist only as a brain in a vat. Imagine, then, that my belief that I am looking at a lemon is caused by an evil scientist who is stimulating my brain with electrodes. The internalist would claim that so long as the brain processes caused by the scientist are the same as the brain processes that would have been caused by actually seeing a lemon, I come to have the same belief. From my perspective there would certainly be no difference. Thus, the causal origins of my belief that I am looking at a lemon are very important for determining whether my belief is true or false, but those causal origins do not determine the *content* of my belief. The content is dependent on what happens in my brain.

Two Arguments for Externalism

Although it was originally intended as a defence for a particular theory of meaning, the best known argument for externalism comes from Hilary Putnam's **Twin Earth** thought experiment. The thought experiment asks us to imagine that in addition to Earth there is a place called Twin Earth. Twin Earth is exactly like Earth in almost every respect. In fact, each of us has a twin on Twin Earth who leads the same life we do, performs all the same actions, is physically indistinguishable from us, and even speaks English. There is, however, one minor difference between Earth and Twin Earth. On Twin Earth the stuff they call "water" that fills the lakes and streams and runs out of their faucets is not H_2O, but an entirely different chemical compound that we will abbreviate as XYZ. H_2O and XYZ look and feel exactly the same and even behave the same chemically; without an electron microscope one could not tell the difference between a sample of H_2O and XYZ.

Now suppose Byron and his twin each look at a lake in their respective worlds. By hypothesis, they are in the same brain state (ignoring, for the moment, the fact that Twin-Byron's brain is made mostly of XYZ while Byron's brain is composed mostly of H_2O), and they both have the same kind of visual experience. That is, what is happening in Byron's and Twin-Byron's head is exactly the same, and the way the lake *looks* to each of them is identical; they have qualitatively indistinguishable experiences. Furthermore, each of them might think to himself "Water looks so refreshing." In one sense it would appear as though Byron and his twin are in the same mental state, for what is going on in their heads is identical. However, on Earth water is H_2O while on Twin Earth water is XYZ, so it seems we should say that Byron's thoughts are about H_2O, whereas Twin-Byron's thoughts are about XYZ. In that case, Byron and his twin have thoughts with different contents even though they are in identical brain states.

Think about it this way. Imagine you visited Twin Earth and were offered a glass of water. You might think to yourself "That's a glass of water." Since the glass contains XYZ and not H_2O, your belief would be false. Now suppose you eventually learn that the stuff they call "water" on Twin Earth is really XYZ. You would naturally conclude that on Twin Earth the word "water" has a different meaning from the one it has on Earth. You might mark this difference by saying that on Twin Earth "water" means twin-water. That is, when a Twin Earthling says "Cold water is good for removing blood stains," he means that cold twin-water is good for removing blood stains. You would also take this utterance to indicate that he *believes* that twin-water is good for removing blood stains. This is a distinct belief from the one his twin on Earth would have. On Earth the claim "Cold water is good for removing blood stains" means cold *water* is good for removing blood stains. When an Earthling says this he is expressing his belief that cold *water* (not cold twin-water) is good for removing blood stains. Thus, despite the fact that these two individuals are physically identical and utter the same sentences, their beliefs have different contents. Earthlings and their twins therefore have different beliefs, but the difference is not due to differences in their neurology (or any other intrinsic difference), it is due entirely to features of the external environment. In this case, then, we have some reason to prefer externalism over internalism.

A second influential argument for externalism, originally formulated by Tyler Burge, focuses on the role of a speech community in determining mental content. Burge asks us to imagine two scenarios. The first involves Janis, who has had arthritis in her hands for a number of years. We will assume that she is as familiar as the average person with arthritis and, for the most part, uses the word "arthritis" properly in everyday conversation. For instance, she says things like "I have arthritis in my hands," "There is a history of arthritis in my family," and "My hands hurt because I have arthritis." Let us also suppose that one day she starts having a pain in her thigh that feels very much like the pain in her hands. She is disturbed by this, goes to her doctor, and informs her that she is afraid her arthritis has spread to her thigh. Janis's doctor tells her that this is impossible because arthritis is an inflammation of the joints; since the thigh is not a joint, the pain must be due to something else.

There are two things to notice about this story. First, although Janis is a competent speaker of English, she did not fully understand the meaning of the word "arthritis." If she were aware of the dictionary definition, she would not have believed that she had arthritis in her thigh. This kind of mistake is, of course, quite common. Few of us have the lexicographer's command of a language, and so we misuse words on a regular basis. The second thing we should note is that Janis really did believe that she had arthritis in her thigh, but that her belief was false since it is impossible to have arthritis in any part of the body except the joints.

In the second scenario Burge asks us to imagine that everything happens just as it did in the first, except that Janis's linguistic community is different. In the alternative speech community the word "arthritis" means an inflammation that can occur in joints *and* elsewhere in the body. In this case, then, it *is* possible to have arthritis in one's thigh. Since the meaning of the word "arthritis" differs in these two speech communities, we would need to translate "arthritis" in the second community as a word that differs from our word "arthritis"; let's call it "shmarthritis." In light of this, our second story turns out rather differently from the first: Janis does not use the word "arthritis" improperly, and her belief that she has arthritis in her thigh is true. But does Janis have the *same belief* in both of these stories? According to Burge she does not. In the first case her belief is about arthritis, an inflammation of the joints; in the second case her belief is about shmarthritis, a different kind of inflammation that can occur in the thigh. The contents of Janis's beliefs are therefore different in our two stories, but what accounts for this difference?

By the terms of Burge's thought experiment there are no intrinsic differences between Janis in the first story and in the second. In either case she suffers from the same physical afflic-tion, she behaves in the same way, and she makes all the same utterances. For instance, she says "I believe I have arthritis in my thigh" in both stories. We are also supposed to assume that Janis's brain states are the same in both situations. The only difference lies in the linguistic practices of Janis's community. The use of the word "arthritis" is different in the first situation than the second, and this difference seems to affect the content of Janis's beliefs. Once again, then, we have reason to believe that the content of one's thoughts depends on more than one's brain states; mental content can also depend on the conven-tions of one's linguistic community. If this is right, then it appears we have further reason to believe externalism is correct.

Although the details of Burge's and Putnam's arguments are quite different, the form of their arguments is exactly the same. In both cases we are asked to imagine two individuals who have all the same intrinsic properties (e.g., the same brain states and behaviour) but who differ in one of their relational properties (to H_2O or XYZ; to different sets of linguistic practices). In light of the relational differences we are to conclude that the individuals in question have different beliefs. Since the differences in mental content stem from relational and not intrinsic differences, externalism must be true; mental content does in fact depend crucially on features outside the thinker.

Despite the similarity between Putnam's and Burge's arguments, there is some reason to prefer Burge's approach over Putnam's. First, Burge's argument is more plausible since it does not require anything as fanciful as Twin Earth or something as fantastic as a chemical compound that behaves exactly like H_2O but is an entirely different substance. Second, and more significantly, it is unclear that the Twin Earth argument can be generalized in a way that supports externalism about all, or even most, mental states. The argument depends crucially on the possibility of two qualitatively indiscernible things that have fundamentally different objective natures (that is, on Twin Earth *all* water is XYZ and on Earth *all* water is H_2O). While this possibility might justify externalism for mental states about water and other kinds of substances with similar objective natures such as gold or carbon (these are often called *natural kinds*), it is difficult to see how this might work for beliefs about things like chairs or corkscrews. It seems more difficult to run an analogous argument about chairs or corkscrews because chairs and corkscrews do not appear to have a mandatory objective nature (that is, chairs and corkscrews are not all the same on either Earth or Twin Earth since they can be made of entirely different substances). If we were limited to the Putnam-style argument, although it is clear that we should be externalists about mental states that involve natural kinds like gold and water, we might have to be internalists about all other mental states.

Although this might be the view one should adopt, externalists generally find Burge's argument more attractive because it extends more readily to a broader range of mental states than Putnam's. It is not very difficult to imagine that our linguistic practices might have been different from how they actually are, so it is a simple matter to formulate other arguments analogous to the arthritis example about almost anything. For instance, we could imagine that the word "chair" referred only to the sub-class of chairs with arms and that we call chairs without arms "shmairs." Suppose, then, that I am sitting on a chair without arms. In the actual world you might think, truly, that I am sitting on a comfortable chair. Now imagine that in our alternative situation you are unaware of the difference between "chairs" and "shmairs" and think in an identical situation that I am sitting on a comfortable chair. In this case your belief would be false and would have different content from your belief in the actual world. Of course, the only difference between these two hypothetical situations is the linguistic practice of the community in which you exist. Assuming this style of argument is convincing, it seems to support a more thorough form of externalism than Putnam's, for we could use it with *any* concept, so long as there is the possibility of a speaker misusing that concept.

While these kinds of arguments are plausible and have been extremely influential, externalism often appears to be a strange and unlikely view. One of the attractive features of internalism is that it has a fairly straightforward answer to the question

"Where are a person's mental states?" Internalists claim the answer is "In the head" or "In the brain," which is intuitively appealing, especially for identity theorists like the ones we discussed in earlier chapters. According to externalists, however, the answer to this question is "Out there in the world," or "Out there in your linguistic community." This is likely to strike you as a very odd suggestion. While it is palatable to many to claim that a mental state like the belief that water is wet is really a brain state, it is surely very strange to say that this belief is in large part constituted by the water in the thinker's environment or by a certain set of linguistic practices. Do we really want to say that my thought about the world is composed by the world itself? In the next section we will examine two arguments against externalism and in favour of internalism.

Two Arguments for Internalism

There are two compelling arguments against externalism, both of which point out that externalism has some undesirable implications which would be avoided if we adopted internalism instead. The first argument points out that if externalism were true it would undermine the idea that, generally speaking, we know the contents of our own minds. The second, which is more complex, claims that externalism does not allow mental content to play a causal role in our behaviour. Let's consider each of these in turn.

Conventional wisdom tells us that you know the contents of your own mind. In part, this is related to the fact that the kind of access you have to your mind is different from the access others have; yours is more immediate and reliable. Let's assume you believe it is raining outside. I might be able to conclude on the basis of certain behavioural evidence that you have this belief, but I could never be certain. Perhaps you are just *pretending* to believe it is raining, or perhaps you *always* wear a raincoat. Your access to this belief is entirely different, however. You do not need to check to see if you believe that it is raining or draw inferences based on your own behaviour, you just know you believe it by thinking it. This is not to say that your knowledge of the contents of your own mind is incorrigible. It is possible to make mistakes. Freud has shown us that we are sometimes unaware of some of our deepest (and darkest) thoughts and desires, and that sometimes we think we believe or desire one thing when in fact we really believe or desire something else. But while it is undoubtedly true that sometimes you don't know the contents of your own mind, this is surely the exception rather than the rule. Most of the time you know directly and perfectly well what you believe and desire.

Externalism threatens conventional wisdom on this matter. One of the implications of externalism is that we might not know what we believe. To illustrate the problem, let's revisit Putnam's Twin Earth thought experiment and add a twist. Imagine you are an astronaut and that rapid transit between planets is possible. Let's also imagine that you travel regularly between Earth and Twin Earth. Because you spend equal amounts of time on each planet, your thoughts and speech fall into line with the local inhabitants. That is, when you are on Twin Earth you have twin-water thoughts about XYZ, and when you are on Earth you have water thoughts about H_2O.

Since you go back and forth between these two planets so often, and since they look exactly the same, it is inevitable that at some point you will forget which planet you are on. On some occasion, then, you will think you are on Twin Earth but are actually on Earth. Suppose this happens and you think to yourself "I would like a glass of water." According to externalism, as we have seen, the content of this thought is crucially dependent on the environment—on whether it includes *water* or *twin-water*. Since you don't know which planet you are on, you do not have access to the relevant information about your environment. It follows, then, that you don't know whether you believe that you would like a glass of water or a glass of twin-water. Even while you consciously have this belief, you do not know its content. To find out what you believe you would need to run a test on some water and discover whether it is H_2O or XYZ.

This is certainly a counterintuitive conclusion, but it does seem to follow from an externalist theory of content. If, as Burge suggests, *most* of our thoughts get their contents from factors outside our bodies (such as our linguistic community), we cannot tell just by introspecting our mental states what we believe. That is, I cannot, simply by turning my attention to *my own thoughts*, tell whether I live in a world with water or twin-water, or in a world with one set of linguistic practices as opposed to another. Thus, if the externalist theory of content is true for most of our mental states, we do not know the contents of most of our thoughts. This leads to a new and strange version of the problem of other minds we discussed in Chapter 2. The difference is that the new version of the problem concerns knowledge of *one's own mind* as opposed to the minds of *others.* Internalists claim that this is too high a price to pay for a theory of content. If we cannot be certain of the contents of our own minds, it is hard to see how we could be certain of anything. Externalism, then, opens the door to an unpalatable form of scepticism, and this is reason enough to adopt internalism instead.

The second argument against externalism involves the conviction that our mental states have a causal role to play in the production of our behaviour. In Chapter 5 we observed that when two events are causally related it is natural to assume that the cause produces the effect in virtue of possessing certain properties. For instance, if the impact of a brick against a window causes the window to break, it is presumably certain properties of the brick (or of its impact with the window) rather than others that contribute to this particular effect. The velocity, direction, and density of the brick are no doubt causally significant, whereas its colour, the fact the brick was once part of a wall, or was played with by a child ten years ago, are not. That is to say, the brick would have broken the window just the same even if it had been a different colour, had never been part of a wall, or had never been played with.

The properties mentioned above include both intrinsic and relational varieties. While some of the intrinsic properties are causally relevant and others are not, it is clear that none of the relational properties mentioned played a role in causing the window to break. In fact, it is difficult to see how *any* relational property of the brick could matter to what the cause produces. What seems important is what the brick itself was like as opposed to the various relations the brick had to other things. The lesson we might draw from this is that only the intrinsic properties of a cause (or a sub-class of them) have a role to play in bringing about an effect, in which case the relational properties of a cause are always causally irrelevant.

Imagine that your chair suddenly catches fire. You believe that the glass next to you contains water, so you pour it over the flames and thereby avert disaster. Your action (pouring out the water) undoubtedly has very complex causal origins which we might explain in the following way. Taking hold of the glass and pouring out the water is a movement that involves various muscles, which were put into motion by nerve signals sent from your brain. Those nerve signals were presumably caused by other brain states the causal origins of which can be traced back to the brain state that is identical with or otherwise causally related to your believing that the glass in question contained water. In any case, the fact you believed the glass contained water seems to be a significant causal factor in your action. Had you thought the glass was full of gasoline, you would (I hope) have acted differently.

If externalism is correct, the content of your belief is not a property of your brain or central nervous system; it is (in part) a relationship between you and water. This creates a serious complication for the causal story sketched out above. We have seen that only the intrinsic properties of an event have a causal role to play in what that event causes. If mental content is a relational property as the externalist claims, then it cannot play any causal role in behaviour. This means the fact you believed the glass contained water was *irrelevant* to your action, which is a very odd conclusion, for the fact you thought the glass contained water seemed to be crucial to explaining your behaviour. At a more general level, denying that mental content plays a causal role in our behaviour implies that we can never explain our behaviour by appealing to the content of our mental states. The internalist would point out that this is an absurd state of affairs, for our ordinary explanatory practices strongly indicate otherwise. Most of the time, explaining human behaviour is *precisely* a matter of identifying what people think, believe, fear, or desire, and all these states explain *in virtue* of their mental content.

This problem can be avoided if one rejects externalism and adopts an internalist model of mental content instead. To return to the example above, if the content of your belief that the glass next to you contains water is identical to a certain brain state, it is a simple matter to fit that content into the causal story we sketched out earlier: the brain state initiates a sequence of neural events that sends signals to your arm that cause the muscles in your arm and hand to move in such a way as to pick up the glass and pour the water onto the fire. Thus, internalism rather than externalism appears to be more compatible with our practice of explaining human behaviour by appealing to mental content.

We have seen, then, that internalism and externalism each have their merits and their shortcomings. You should not, however, have the impression that you must choose one theory over the other. As we noted in our discussion of Putnam and Burge, it is possible to be an externalist about some mental content and an internalist about the rest. If we are careful about what kinds of content are internalist and what kinds are externalist, perhaps the problems we have identified would be minimized.

Broad and Narrow Content

Another approach to the problems we have discussed is to propose that there are two *kinds* of content and that all (or most) mental states possess *both* varieties. Mental content that is determined according to internalist criteria is called **narrow content**, whereas content that is determined by externalist criteria is called **broad content**. Even if one finds the arguments for externalism compelling, it is difficult to deny that there is something important that is shared by Earthlings and Twin Earthlings or by Janis in her two possible speech communities; their subjective points of view are the same. That is, things *seem the same* to the inhabitants of Earth and Twin Earth when they think about water and twin-water: they both think about a liquid that is tasteless, transparent, and odourless; what they each call "water" has the same conceptual significance for the inhabitants of both worlds. Thus, even though we might want to say that on Earth the thought that water is wet is about H_2O and that on Twin Earth it is about XYZ, there is a kind of content that is common to both thoughts. This common element is narrow content.

If this kind of distinction makes sense, it might be possible to address the problems with externalism in the following way. While we cannot know the broad contents of our own thoughts through introspection, we do know their narrow contents. Thus, although our astronaut who travels between Earth and Twin Earth does not know whether his belief is about water or twin-water, he at least knows that it is about *watery stuff*. While this is not without its problems, such an approach would seem to avert the peculiar form of scepticism identified earlier and fits with the common conviction that the contents of our own minds are not a mystery. Furthermore, we might say that although broad contents do not make a causal contribution to our behaviour, narrow contents do. Perhaps all that is required to explain your pouring of the water on the fire is the fact you believed the glass contained watery stuff. Since this content is narrow and can be identified with a brain state, the causal argument against externalism is also avoided. While this is an appealing proposal, it is unclear how effective the distinction between broad and narrow content is at circumventing the traditional problems with externalism. Philosophers remain divided on this issue, and many doubt that broad content is really a form of content at all.

Suggestions for Further Reading

Burge, T. 1979. "Individualism and the Mental." *Midwest Studies in Philosophy* 4.

Kim, J. 1996. "Mental Content." *Philosophy of Mind.* Boulder, CO: Westview Press.

Putnam, H. 1975. "The Meaning of 'Meaning.'" *Language, Mind, and Knowledge.* Ed. K. Gunderson. Minneapolis, MN: University of Minnesota Press.

Seager, W. 1999. *Theories of Consciousness: An Introduction and Assessment.* London: Routledge.

■ THE PROBLEM OF QUALIA

Qualia and the Problem of Consciousness

Qualia (often also referred to as *phenomenal properties*) are the subjective aspects of experience, the way sensations *feel* to those who have them. Qualia are the painfulness of pains, the sweetness of sugar, and the redness of red, to name just a few examples. Taken collectively, qualia make up the bulk of what we refer to as **consciousness**, for being conscious is usually a matter of being aware of the sweetness of sugar, the redness of red, and so on. We have already seen that these properties can be a thorn in the side of physicalist theories. Behaviourism seemed inadequate in part because it ignored the subjective character of sensations by reducing them to mere behavioural dispositions. The type identity theory got into trouble because it seemed to imply that physically diverse creatures could not have the same kind of qualia. Functionalism looked unappealing because it placed qualia on the sideline by claiming that the subjective characters of our sensations play no role in their identity; for example, saying that the sensation of red would remain the sensation of red even if it *felt* like a sensation of green. In this final chapter we will explore the view that qualia undermine *all* forms of physicalism. We will ease our way into this discussion with a brief examination of Thomas Nagel's reflections on the nature of subjectivity. Once we have clarified Nagel's concerns, we will explore and evaluate Frank Jackson's direct assault against physicalism and determine what implications, if any, may be drawn from qualia for the mind-body problem.

What is it like to be Conscious?

In his famous article "What is it Like to Be a Bat?" Thomas Nagel argues that consciousness is a serious obstacle for philosophers who wish to advance a physicalist theory of mind. In spite of his belief in the seriousness of this obstacle, Nagel falls short of saying that physicalism is false. Instead, he claims that consciousness poses a problem to our ability to *understand how physicalism could be true.* Thus, we should not take his argument to be a rejection of physicalism in favour of dualism, but as an expression of our own ignorance about how consciousness could be a physical phenomenon.

Before exploring Nagel's argument, we need to appreciate his understanding of consciousness. He sums up what it is to be conscious in the following way: if something is conscious, then *there is something it is like to be that thing.* To be conscious is to have subjectivity; that is, to experience the world in a particular way. The items that make up consciousness are the qualia associated with individual experiences or sensations, each of which has its own felt subjective character. Nagel proposes that consciousness is probably something that admits of degrees and exists in a variety of different animal species, perhaps even in unimaginable forms of life on distant planets. For example, if we suppose that bats are conscious, then we are saying that there is something it is like to be a bat. This will include, among other things, what it is like to hang upside down in a dark place all day, what it is like to locate an insect in mid-flight using echolocation, and so on.

Now suppose that you want to know what it is like to be a bat. The fact that bats have a perceptual system that is very different from yours makes it difficult. While it is true that you can *imagine* what it is like to hang upside down or to detect and capture insects while flying at night, this only tells you what it would be like for *you* to be a bat, not what it is like *for a bat* to be a bat. That is, when you imagine hanging upside down or detecting insects with sound waves, you are imagining *yourself* doing this, but you are a human being and not a bat, so there is undoubtedly something that your imagination does not adequately capture. If your imagination can't help you learn what it is like to be a bat, then perhaps science can. Maybe if you studied the brains and perceptual mechanisms of bats and learned all the details about how they function, then you would know what it is like to be a bat. According to Nagel, this is of no help either. The problem is that to understand what it is like to be a bat requires you to adopt a bat's point of view, but studying how a bat's perceptual system functions is not adopting a bat's point of view; it is to take a human point of view of a bat's physiology.

This seems like a fairly simple observation about bat consciousness but actually has profound implications for the mind-body problem when we generalize the claim about bat consciousness to claims about consciousness itself. If certain facts about consciousness are accessible only from a particular point of view (i.e., the first-person point of view of the conscious subject), then it is hard to see how the true nature of consciousness could be revealed by an analysis of a conscious being's neurophysiology. When physicalists tell us that consciousness is a brain state, a functional state, or some other kind of physical state, they purport to be telling us what consciousness *really is*; they are identifying the **objective nature of consciousness**. A physical analysis of consciousness, though, requires us to abandon the point of view of the conscious subject (the first-person point of view) in favour of a third-person, scientific perspective. To return to Nagel's example, if bat consciousness is defined in relation to the bat's point of view, then studying a bat's neurophysiology is, by definition, to abandon the bat's point of view. If this is true, then it seems that studying a bat's brain and perceptual system cannot be the study of a bat's consciousness. By analogy, the study of the human brain and perceptual system cannot reveal the true nature of consciousness either. To study the physical processes involved in thought and perception is to abandon the first-person point of view that defines consciousness.

To grasp fully the nature of the problem, Nagel contrasts the attempt to provide an objective, scientific characterization of a phenomenon like lightning with the attempt to provide an objective, scientific characterization of consciousness. Lightning has an objective nature that is not necessarily revealed in our perceptual experiences of it. We see lightning as a bright flash of light in the sky. However, other creatures might perceive it quite differently. For example, Martians might be able to detect lightning as an ultraviolet flash, which is beyond our visual range. Although humans and Martians detect lightning differently, this is no obstacle to our agreeing on an objective characterization of lightning. We can both agree that lightning is a rapid electrical discharge without agreeing about how lightning appears to us perceptually. What our agreement about the nature of lightning consists in is a conceptual movement from our own *subjective* points of view on lightning (for humans, a bright blue-white flash of light in the sky; for Martians, an ultraviolet flash) toward an understanding that is *not associated with any particular point of view.*

The attempt to provide an objective characterization of consciousness faces a challenge that does not exist in the case of lightning. The nature of lightning is not something that has to be understood from a particular (first-person) perspective—in fact, the point is *not* to understand it from any *particular* perspective—which is why it is so easy for us and our Martian friends to agree about what lightning really is. The nature of consciousness, however, *is* something that has to be understood from a particular perspective, for it *is* the taking of a first-person perspective on the world since consciousness is *what it is like to be that conscious creature.*

As we saw, a physicalist understanding of any phenomenon, including consciousness, requires giving up the point of view of the conscious subject, but if we abandon this, have we not thereby ceased to talk about consciousness? Haven't we just changed the subject? In Nagel's view, these observations lead to a dilemma. If physicalism is true, there must be an objective, physical description of subjectivity. However, the more objective a point of view one takes toward consciousness, the further away one moves from the subjectivity that defines consciousness.

Nagel confesses that as yet he sees no way out of this dilemma. On the one hand, he is very sympathetic with physicalism, in which case he thinks there must be an objective, physical description of consciousness. On the other hand, he doesn't see how one could understand consciousness in physical terms without abandoning the subjectivity that makes consciousness what it is. To say that there is currently no way to resolve this dilemma is not to say that it can *never* be resolved. Nagel proposes that there might come a time when we will develop concepts that will enable us to understand how consciousness could be a physical phenomenon.

To illustrate why there might be reason for optimism about this issue, let's consider an analogy. Most of us have heard the expression "matter is energy." In the twelfth century it is most likely that such a claim would have been regarded either as meaningless or as false. Even today, most of us have only a vague idea of what it means. However, there *are* people alive today who understand this claim perfectly. The reason they understand the claim "matter is energy" and people in the twelfth century (and many of us today) did not is because it is only in the light of a certain kind of background knowledge that the claim "matter is energy" can make any sense. Knowing what this claim means requires knowledge of a branch of theoretical physics that didn't exist in the twelfth century and with which very few of us are acquainted today.

Nagel speculates that one day we might possess a new theoretical background that will enable us to understand the claim "consciousness is a physical phenomenon" in the way a background in modern physics enables people to understand the claim "matter is energy." Right now the claim about consciousness is to us as the claim about matter and energy was to people in the twelfth century. Nagel's optimism, of course, depends on what is possible, and it is difficult to say whether or not the prospects for the development of the new theoretical background are high or low. It could turn out that a pessimistic attitude toward the problem of consciousness is more appropriate. It could be the case that we will never possess the cognitive abilities required to make sense of physicalism.

The Knowledge Argument

We saw that Nagel's argument was not intended to undermine the truth of physicalism but to show that there is a profound conceptual obstacle to our ability to understand how qualia could be physical properties. Frank Jackson also thinks that qualia create a special problem for physicalism but he argues for a more radical conclusion. In his view, the reality of qualia implies the falsity of physicalism and the truth of a form of dualism. The form of dualism in question is not a dualism of substances like Descartes's, but rather a dualism of *properties*. Jackson argues that qualia are non-physical properties of the brain, and furthermore, he argues that these properties are epiphenomenal.

Jackson justifies these two conclusions with what he calls the **knowledge argument**. Although there are actually two versions of the knowledge argument, we will focus on one of them only. Jackson asks us to imagine Mary, a woman who has never seen colours. The reason Mary has never seen colour is unimportant. Perhaps she has been imprisoned in a black and white environment for her entire life and her skin and eyes have been dyed shades of pale grey, or perhaps she was surgically altered at birth in a way that rendered her unable to see colours. Whatever the reason, Mary has only seen the world in black, white, and shades of grey. Despite Mary's lack of colour experiences, she becomes the world's most accomplished neurophysiologist. In fact, Mary's knowledge is so extensive that she knows *all* the physical facts about colour vision. This is clearly a great deal more than what anyone *actually* knows about the physical processes involved in colour vision and perhaps also more than anyone with limited memory and intelligence *could* know. Mary knows everything physical *there is to know* about such processes, so that her knowledge is *exhaustive*. Thus, we need to imagine that Mary knows what all the physical effects will be when someone with normal vision looks at any coloured object. She knows what wave lengths of light stimulate which rods and cones in the retinas, what effect this stimulation has on the brain, and can even explain down to the smallest physical detail how these events eventually produce the utterance "That's blue." Furthermore, since Mary's knowledge is so vast, she can even predict with perfect accuracy how normal people will react to colour.

Once we have imagined Mary having all this knowledge at her disposal, Jackson asks us to imagine that she escapes from her black and white environment or is surgically altered so that she can have colour experiences just like everybody else. Now suppose that Mary's first colour experience is of the sky. For the very first time Mary sees the sky the way other people do; she has a sensation of blue. Jackson asks us to consider the following question: does Mary learn something new when she sees blue for the first time?

You probably think she does, and Jackson agrees. What is it that Mary learns? The most obvious answer is that Mary learns what it is like to see blue. Before her new-found ability to see colour, she knew what happens in peoples' brains and central nervous systems when they look at blue objects, but none of this told her *what it is like to see blue*. This is a fact that eluded her until she had a sensation of blue for herself. If we agree with Jackson on this point, it seems that physicalism is in trouble. What Mary learns must either be a physical fact or a non-physical fact. We have already said that Mary knew all the physical facts about colour experience before she saw colours for herself. If what it is like to see blue were just another in a long list of physical facts about colour perception, then it is something Mary would have known already. Thus, if we agree with Jackson that Mary learns a new fact, what she learns must be a *non-physical fact*. If there are non-physical facts it follows that physicalism is false, for physicalism denies that there are any such facts. The knowledge argument, then, proves that colour qualia, such as the felt blueness of sensations caused by the sky, are *non-physical properties*. If they weren't, then Mary would have known about them all along.

Jackson claims that the knowledge argument shows not only that qualia are non-physical, but also that they are *epiphenomenal*. We have already encountered epiphenomenalism in Chapter 1 and again in Chapter 5. There we learned that to say something is epiphenomenal is to deny that it makes any causal contribution to the world. When Jackson claims that qualia are epiphenomenal, he is therefore saying that they are without any causal influence. Thus, when Mary says something like, "So *that's* what blue looks like!" when she first looks at the sky after her operation, it is not the blueness of her sensation that causes her to make this utterance. Instead, Mary says what she does in virtue of the physical processes happening in her body.

The reason Jackson thinks qualia are epiphenomenal has to do with the fact that Mary's knowledge of the physical causes and effects of colour experience was complete. Mary could provide a causal explanation down to the smallest detail for why someone utters "That's red" in the presence of a red object. If non-physical properties played a causal role at some point in the sequence of causes and effects that produce this utterance, Mary would have noticed causal interventions by a mysterious force she could not identify or explain. Since, by hypothesis, Mary notices no such mysterious causal interventions, qualia must not make any causal contribution to the processes that lead to the identified behaviour.

To clarify this line of reasoning, consider the following example. Imagine you are a forensic scientist studying a footprint in clay. Given a shoe and asked to determine if it made the footprint, you try to match the shape and size of the print to the shape and size of the sole of the shoe. What you are trying to determine is whether or not the shoe *caused* the footprint. If the sole and the footprint match perfectly, then you have fully explained the cause of the footprint and have accounted for its width, breadth, depth, and shape. In this case, the physical features of the sole of the shoe *completely explain* the physical features of the footprint. But now imagine that in addition to the shoe some other causal factor contributed to the properties of the footprint. In this case, the properties of the shoe would not tell the complete story about the footprint; there would be properties of the footprint that are not explained by the properties of the shoe. If you are doing your job properly, you should conclude that the shoe played a significant causal role in the production of the footprint, but that something else you are not able to identify also played a causal role.

This analogy should help us to appreciate that if something Mary didn't know about (i.e., non-physical qualia) played a causal role in peoples' behaviour toward coloured objects, she would have recognized that her causal account of human behaviour was incomplete. She would have noticed that some missing factor was influencing the causal processes leading to behaviour in the same way the forensic scientist realized that something other than the shoe must have contributed to the shape of the footprint. Since, by hypothesis, Mary notices no such missing factors, qualia cannot make any contribution to our behaviour.

Jackson's knowledge argument bears a strong resemblance to Nagel's argument, so it would be a good idea to clarify the differences between them. The most obvious is the scope of their conclusions. Jackson uses his argument to demonstrate the falsity of physicalism and the truth of dualism. By contrast, Nagel offers a more guarded conclusion to the effect that, although physicalism might be true, we cannot currently understand how this is so. Despite the different conclusions Jackson and Nagel each draw, the arguments themselves can be difficult to distinguish. This is because they both refer to *what it is like* to experience something.

Despite this similarity, however, there is an important difference. At the centre of Nagel's argument is a general claim about the relationship between objectivity and subjectivity. In his view, consciousness *is* subjectivity, which he understands in terms of *what it is like* to be a conscious being. Because Nagel claims that subjectivity must be understood from the point of view of the conscious subject, this appears to preclude the possibility of the scientific study of consciousness, for scientific study abandons the point of view of the conscious subject for an objective point of view. However, Jackson is not particularly concerned with the relationship between subjectivity and objectivity. He argues instead that any physical description of an experience will leave out certain facts about that experience. These are facts about qualia, about what it is like to have that experience. When Jackson says that Mary doesn't know what it is like to see blue before her transformation, he is not saying that she doesn't know *what it is like to be a person who sees blue*; he is saying only that there is a property of sensations of blue to which Mary doesn't have access. Since Mary supposedly has access to all the physical properties of sensation, what she is missing must be a non-physical property.

Reactions to the Knowledge Argument

Jackson's knowledge argument has provoked a great deal of discussion and criticism. In general, the responses to it fall into one of two categories. In one camp are those who think his conclusion seems to follow only because he illicitly exploits our imaginations. In the other camp are those who claim that Mary only acquires a different kind of knowledge of the same old physical facts she knew before.

Daniel Dennett is a representative of the first camp. He claims that the reason many of us find Jackson's argument compelling is that we don't realize that we can't actually do what the argument demands of us. The knowledge argument asks us to imagine that Mary knows all the physical information associated with colour vision. In Dennett's view, this is simply beyond the scope of what we can imagine. The best any of us can do is to imagine that Mary knows an awful lot about the neurophysiology of visual experience, for we have no idea what having *all* the physical information would involve. This, of course, falls significantly short of imagining that Mary knows all the physical information. The significance of this, according to Dennett, is that if we could successfully imagine Mary having all the physical information, we might not think that Mary learns anything new when she first sees colours. If we could really imagine what is involved in knowing everything physical there is to know about colour vision, it might have been obvious to us from the beginning that Mary would also have known what it is like to see colour, even before her transformation.

The second critique, exemplified by Paul Churchland, simply denies that Mary learns a new fact when she first sees colours. According to Churchland, when Mary first sees colours she does not learn any new information, she just comes to know familiar facts in a new way. Thus, *what* Mary knows is the same before and after her corrective surgery; all that changes is her *way* of knowing it. Before Mary saw colour she knew everything physical about colour experience, including every single neurological event that is involved in colour processing. However, since Mary never saw colour herself until her corrective operation, her own brain was never in the physical state that other people's brains were in when they experienced colours. In Churchland's view, when Mary finally sees colour, the only thing that changes is that her *own brain* finally enters the physical state she previously observed only in other people. The reason we find it plausible to say that Mary learns something new (i.e., what it is like to see colour) has nothing to do with her learning a new fact. The apparent difference in Mary's knowledge can be completely explained by pointing out that Mary now has a different kind of access to the physical facts she knew before. She was able only to observe the sensation of blue by studying the brains of others using scientific instruments, but now that her own brain is capable of having this sensation, she can access the sensation of blue by introspecting her own brain states. What changes about Mary, then, is that she acquires a new kind of knowledge, but she does not thereby learn new facts.

The difference Churchland appeals to is not unlike the distinction between **knowledge by description** and **knowledge by acquaintance**. Suppose that you have never been to Hong Kong but that it is a place that has always fascinated you. You might read lots of books about Hong Kong and study maps and photographs, and thereby learn all about the city. Thus, you can be said to *know* Hong Kong without ever going there. Now imagine that you save enough money for the trip and finally travel to Hong Kong. Things are likely to seem different to you while visiting Hong Kong than when you merely read about it and looked at pictures. However, this does not necessarily mean that you learn anything new about Hong Kong. *What* you know (i.e., Hong Kong) is the same in either case. All that has changed is your *way of knowing* Hong Kong. Before, you knew Hong Kong by description and now you know it by acquaintance, for to visit Hong Kong is to become *acquainted* with the city. The parallel with Mary is that before her corrective operation she knew sensations of colour by description, and after the operation she comes to know sensations of colour by acquaintance. *What* she knows is the same thing in either case (i.e., some kind of brain state), but her *way* of knowing it changes. For the knowledge argument to work we need to be convinced that Mary learns new facts about colour experience. The knowledge argument relies on a fairly strong intuition that there is a significant difference in Mary's experience before and after she sees colours for the first time, a difference that can only be explained by saying that Mary learns new facts. Churchland's method of undermining the argument is to provide an alternative account of the difference in Mary's knowledge without appealing to any new facts. He says that all that changes is Mary's *way of knowing* sensations of colour. If he is correct and Mary doesn't learn new *facts* when she first sees colour, there is no reason to believe there are non-physical facts, in which case Jackson's conclusion is left without any support.

Dennett's and Churchland's objections deal with the conclusion that qualia are non-physical, but what shall we say about Jackson's argument for the other conclusion: i.e., that qualia are *epiphenomenal*? This may be vulnerable to a charge of inconsistency. Here's the problem. What is it that you imagine when (or if) you find it so obvious that Mary learns something new when she sees colours for the first time? You probably imagine her looking at the world around her in a state of wonder and picture her saying things like "I never dreamed that red would look like *that*!" You imagine that she expresses wonder at her first sunset, that she is suddenly able to sort orange from red objects without her colour-detecting instruments, that she says how happy she is that she can finally see what colours are like, and that she says she never dreamed that she was missing so much. In general, then, you imagine Mary's *behaviour* being altered in ways like these. So now let's ask why you think Mary would behave differently after her introduction to the coloured world. You must assume that her new-found colour qualia have an effect on Mary's behaviour. That is, the reason you think Mary would say "I never dreamed that red would look like *that*!" is because you assume that the redness of her experience causes her to say that. This seems quite natural, and, indeed, there is good reason to suppose that it is precisely this line of reasoning that leads most readers of the knowledge argument to the conclusion that Mary learns new facts. This is not a problem in itself, but becomes one when Jackson claims that the knowledge argument demonstrates that qualia are epiphenomenal.

This claim is inconsistent with the knowledge argument if the argument depends on the assumption that qualia have causal efficacy. To appreciate more clearly that there is, in fact, an inconsistency here, let's imagine for a moment that qualia really are epiphenomenal. This means that colour qualia have no causal influence on *anything*, including Mary's behaviour. If Mary really had all the physical information about colour experience, then she would be able to predict everything she would say and do in the presence of coloured objects. That is, Mary would know exactly what effect a red sunset would have on her brain and central nervous system, right down to all the utterances and bodily movements she would make. If this is so, then could Mary still be surprised when she sees her first sunset? It seems not. She would never express the least bit of surprise or astonishment about her colour experiences, for she knew exactly how she would react beforehand. When the element of surprise and wonder is taken away from Mary's behaviour, it is no longer so obvious that she learns something new when she has her first colour experiences. Our relative certainty that Mary learns something new depends on her being surprised and astonished, so when we take these things away we can't be confident that she learns new facts, in which case we have no reason to think there are non-physical facts. Thus, the problem with Jackson's argument comes to this: if qualia were truly epiphenomenal we would have no reason to think Mary learns new facts, in which case we have no reason to think that qualia are non-physical, epiphenomenal properties.

Is Dualism the Answer?

It is unclear how effective these responses are to Jackson's knowledge argument. While they are persuasive, it is natural to have lingering doubts about whether or not it is possible to capture what it is like to have an experience in physical terms. Thus, although one might agree that the knowledge argument is unpersuasive, one might think that Jackson and Nagel are close to an important truth about the subjective character experience. We started this book by examining different versions of dualism and evaluating their merits and philosophical problems. Most of the remaining chapters involved the study of different forms of physicalism, all of which attempt to undermine dualism and to offer more plausible alternatives. As we have seen, none of these theories can be endorsed completely without embarrassment, for each of them has its own problems and disadvantages. After exploring the problem of qualia for physicalism in this chapter, it is tempting to think that there are good philosophical reasons for a return to some form of dualism. Dualism may indeed be the answer, but we need to be careful not to jump to any hasty conclusions. After all, there might be different versions of physicalism yet to consider.

Although the varieties of physicalism we have examined in this text all have their problems, we need to weigh these difficulties against the philosophical problems faced by dualist theories. In general, physicalist theories are at an advantage because they are simpler than dualist theories. The relative simplicity of any form of physicalism is a consequence of the fact that it has fewer ontological commitments. Dualists think there are two kinds of things in the world—physical things and non-physical things—whereas physicalists believe there are only physical things. As we saw, accepting dualism introduces problems that don't arise for physicalist theories. One must account for the way(s) in which physical and non-physical things are related (or why they seem to be if they are not), and this is a very difficult task since the physical and the non-physical are as different from each other as any two things can be. Interactionism is, although intuitively appealing, philosophically mysterious, and other forms of dualism are philosophically unsatisfying. By contrast, if one is committed to some form of physicalism, an entire cluster of problems does not arise because there are not two distinct kinds of things to relate. On this basis alone, philosophers generally prefer physicalism over dualism, even when they acknowledge that forms of physicalism have philosophical problems.

The entire mind-body problem cannot, however, be decided on the grounds of simplicity and parsimony. Each theory of mind must be evaluated on its own merits and in relation to competing theories. The varieties of physicalism we have explored in this book all have shortcomings, and in one form or another, qualia have consistently been on the list of problems. Does the fact that qualia seem to be a problem for physicalism imply that we should abandon physicalism in favour of dualism? That is one possibility, but one should pause for a moment and consider whether or not dualism can account for qualia any better than physicalism can. Is the nature of subjective experience made any clearer by saying that it is non-physical? Do we understand qualia more if we claim that they are non-physical properties? Do we learn why looking at red feels the way it does if we admit that phenomenal redness is non-physical? It is not obvious that the answer is *yes* to these questions. Most philosophers think that conceding qualia are non-physical properties gets us no closer to understanding them. On the contrary, it appears to make qualia even more mysterious than they already are.

In the end, you will have to decide for yourself which philosophical theories shed light on the nature of mind and which shroud it in additional mystery. Perhaps this consideration, together with questions of internal coherence, ought to guide our choice of the most plausible theory of mind.

Suggestions for Further Reading

Campbell, N. 2003. "An Inconsistency in the Knowledge Argument." *Erkenntnis* 58: 261–66.

Churchland, P. 1985. "Reduction, Qualia, and the Direct Introspection of Brain States." *Journal of Philosophy* 82: 8–28.

Dennett, D. 1991. *Consciousness Explained.* Boston, MA: Little Brown and Co.

Horgan, T. 1984. "Jackson on Physical Information and Qualia." *Philosophical Quarterly* 34: 147–52.

Jackson, F. 1982. "Epiphenomenal Qualia." *Philosophical Quarterly* 32: 127–36.

Jackson, F. 1986. "What Mary Didn't Know." *Journal of Philosophy* 83: 127–36.

McGinn, C. 1989. "Can We Solve the Mind-Body Problem?" *Mind* 98: 349–66.

Nagel, T. 1974. "What Is It Like to Be a Bat?" *Philosophical Review* 83: 435–50.

■ INDEX